Steve Waters

Steve Waters was born in Coventry in 1965. He studied English at Oxford University, taught in secondary schools and was a graduate of David Edgar's MA in Playwriting in 1993, a course which he has run since 2006.

His plays include *English Journeys* (Hampstead Theatre, 1998), *After the Gods* (Hampstead, 2002, published by Faber and Faber), *World Music* (Sheffield Crucible, 2003/Donmar Warehouse, 2004), *The Unthinkable* (Sheffield, 2004), *Fast Labour* (West Yorkshire Playhouse/Hampstead, 2008), *The Contingency Plan* (Bush Theatre, 2009), all of which are published by Nick Hern Books. He also adapted and translated *Habitats* by Philippe Minyana which was staged at the Gate Theatre, London, in 2002 and is published by Oberon Books. Forthcoming work includes *Little Platoons* for the Bush in 2011 and *Amphibians* for Offstage Theatre Company. He has also collaborated with Menagerie Theatre Company, with *Out of Your Knowledge* (2005–8).

Steve has also written extensively for radio and has adapted *The Contingency Plan* for radio and for Film4/Cowboy Films. He has written for the *Guardian*, the *New Statesman* and *Society*, as well as contributing essays to the *Blackwell Companion to Modern British and Irish Drama* and *The Cambridge Companion to Harold Pinter*.

He is a member of the British Theatre Conference.

The Secret Life of Plays

Steve Waters

NICK HERN BOOKS
London
www.nickhernbooks.co.uk

A Nick Hern Book

The Secret Life of Plays
first published in Great Britain in 2010
by Nick Hern Books Limited,
14 Larden Road, London W3 7ST

Cover design by www.energydesignstudio.com

Typeset by Nick Hern Books, London
Printed and bound in Great Britain by
CPI Antony Rowe, Chippenham, Wiltshire

A CIP catalogue record for this book
is available from the British Library

ISBN 978 1 84842 000 7

MIX
Paper from
responsible sources
FSC® C013604

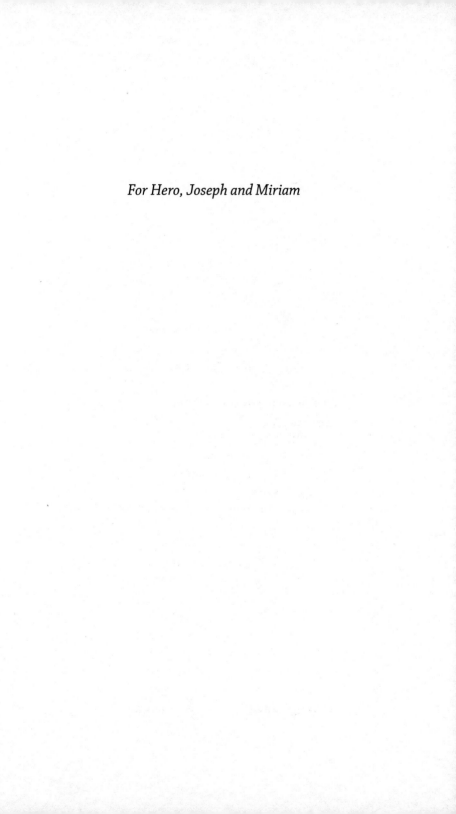

For Hero, Joseph and Miriam

Contents

Acknowledgements

The author and publisher gratefully acknowledge permission to quote from the following:

Attempts on her Life (1997), *The Country* (2000), *The Treatment* (1993) by Martin Crimp; *Translations* by Brian Friel (1981); *Observe the Sons of Ulster Marching Towards the Somme* by Frank McGuinness (1986); *The Birthday Party* (1960), *The Caretaker* (1961), *Old Times* (1971) by Harold Pinter; all published by Faber and Faber Ltd.

Lear (1972), *Saved* (1966) by Edward Bond; *Mother Courage and Her Children* by Bertolt Brecht, translated by John Willett (1980); *Top Girls* by Caryl Churchill (1982); *Copenhagen* by Michael Frayn (1998); *Across Oka* by Robert Holman (1988); *Cleansed* (1998), *Crave* (2001) by Sarah Kane; *Edmond* (1983), *Glengarry Glen Ross* (1984), *Oleanna* (1993) by David Mamet; *The Wonderful World of Dissocia* by Anthony Neilson (2007); *Handbag* by Mark Ravenhill (1998); all published by Methuen Drama, an imprint of A&C Black Publishers Ltd.

Woyzeck by Georg Büchner, translated by Gregory Motton (1991); *Apologia* by Alexi Kaye Campbell (2009); *The Cherry Orchard* by Anton Chekhov, translated by Stephen Mulrine (1998); *Far Away* by Caryl Churchill (2000); *Conversations with Pinter* by Mel Gussow (1995); all published by Nick Hern Books Ltd.

Every effort has been made to contact copyright holders. The publisher will be glad to make good in any future editions any errors or omissions brought to their attention.

Writing this book has made me very aware of the many people to whom I am indebted in terms of my own education in playwriting. I would like to mention with thanks a few of them here, beginning with Professors Valentine Cunningham and Thomas Docherty, and Susan Hitch, who shaped my thinking on so many aspects of this book; to David Edgar himself, without whom it would simply have been an unthinkable project; to the late Clare McIntyre, who taught me the instinctual aspect of the craft and to the also much-missed Sarah Kane, who taught me to rethink everything I thought I had learned hitherto; to my former colleagues at Homerton College, Cambridge, especially Dr Helen Nicholson and Dr Peter Raby, who inducted me into scholarship as an art form; to my friend Ian Smith, whose company and theatrical awareness has informed my own thinking in a multitude of ways; to my former teaching colleagues in numerous schools and especially Simon Veness, who bore the brunt of my very partial theatrical awareness, and to my current colleagues at the University of Birmingham who continue to do so. But most critical of all, to all of those who have been my students across the years in schools, FE colleges, as undergraduates and post-graduates, who have kept the learning alive and vital, and all my comrades as writers and directors in the theatre, and our conversations over the years which have been ruthlessly pillaged here – in particular to Josie Rourke, and my agent and friend Micheline Steinberg. Finally, a debt of love and gratitude is owed to my wife Hero Chalmers, who has encouraged and supported me throughout this project and whose own sharp thinking has been crucial to the outcome; and to my children Joseph and Miriam, who are a daily inspiration.

Last of all I would like to express enormous thanks to my editors at Nick Hern Books and especially to the assiduous and meticulous Robin Booth who has been the kindest and most patient midwife any embryonic author could hope for.

Steve Waters

Introduction
Inside the Apple

'The author is the worm at the core of the apple'
Samuel Beckett

There is something mysterious in the effect and impact of a good play, something that might originate in the intentions of an author, but which soon outstrips them.

As a playwright myself, I recognise the truth of Beckett's image of the place of the author in the act of writing. I have been that 'worm in the apple', excavating my plays from within. [1] My working process is less that of a sculptor, looming over their block of stone in a posture of mastery, and more akin to a miner working their way out from within the rock, hoping to bring some precious metal to light. Plays remain stubbornly paradoxical at their core, beginning as dreams and ending as public documents, as full of space and silence as they are of words and intention.

Most mysterious of all is the very source of a play, the author's intuitive creativity, which resides encrypted in what T.S. Eliot called the 'dark embryo'. If a play doesn't have an umbilical cord feeding into that 'dark embryo', it'll be dead on arrival. And sounding out such sources is unwise. Seamus Heaney characterises the moment of inspiration as being like 'putting your hand into a nest and finding something beginning to hatch out in your head'. What hatches out in the head, not what lurks in the nest, is the concern of this book.

If I begin by recognising the mysteries ahead, it's because all too often writing about playwriting and drama boils down to offering an inventory of conventions, as if plays were no more than the sum of their parts. This approach resembles the attempts of phrenologists to detect a felon from the shape of their skull. In this respect the father of all such commentaries, Aristotle, is culpable in effect, if not intent: how many generations of playwrights and critics have rummaged through the checklist of elements in his *Poetics*, hoping to find there a ready-made framework for their plays? It's all too tempting. Technical terms, especially Greek ones, sound very authoritative: take some *dianoia*, add in a little *sophrosyne*, sprinkle over it a smidgeon of *anagnorisis*, work the whole lot into a lovely *peripeteia*, and wait for the inevitable *katharsis*. It would be unfair to blame this reductiveness on Aristotle alone, whose text was probably a set of lecture notes rather than a more considered work. Nevertheless, his crib set the discussion going and its approach is still mirrored in what there is of playwriting pedagogy today.

Another shortcoming of Aristotle's account of the heyday of Greek theatre is its relentless focus on Sophocles' *Oedipus Tyrannus*. Yes, it's a very good play, no question, but this poster-boy of formal perfection has too often served as a cudgel to beat into shape all sorts of equally good but formally eccentric works. How would Aristotle's toolkit of unities have served him had he considered the unruly danger of Euripides' *The Bacchae* or the trilogy of *The Oresteia*, let alone the madcap playfulness of Aristophanes? The fact that it stakes everything on one exemplary text perhaps explains the seductive reductiveness of the *Poetics*.

Aristotle was primarily a philosopher, and philosophers tend to make dogmatic critics, veering to the prescriptive, dismembering plays to illustrate their concepts. Anyone who has battled with Hegel's writings on tragedy can testify to how theory – even magnificent theory – tends to pare the biodiversity of actual plays back to a monoculture of well-behaved exemplars. Nevertheless, however much we might crave papyrus records of Aeschylus in a post-show discussion, or Euripides' unpublished essays 'Writing in Tavernas', Aristotle's end-of-term report still sets the standard.

And what was written over the next couple of millennia was equally unhelpful. Some nuggets of insight in works largely on rhetoric. A bit of Chaucer. The odd preface to a Ben Jonson play. Tedious cover versions of Aristotle in increasingly dogmatic form by Boileau, Corneille or Dryden. Playwriting reduced to a list of 'don'ts': don't violate unity, don't deviate from decorum, don't mix genres, don't use prose. (Of course, the great plays tumbled out heedless of all this theorising.)

Those who subscribed to the don'ts were largely the dullest dogs. There's a reason why Dryden's rarely revived, why Jonson's rowdy, irregular *Bartholomew Fair* is more to our taste than his tidy *Sejanus*. The well-behaved play – or, as it became known, 'well-made play' – might be one result of following the classicist's rulebook. Of course, if the quantum of passion brought to bear on those rules is equivalent to that which Racine supplied, the results can be electrifying. But it's telling that Shakespeare, now our lodestar, was continually found wanting by philosophers and classicists from Nahum Tate to Dr Johnson, from Voltaire to George Bernard Shaw. Pronouncing him guilty of taking liberties with dramatic form, they duly sentenced him to three centuries of emendation. But Shakespeare's crime was his chief virtue: his raw talent, forging plays through opportunistic plagiarism and visionary innovation.

Shakespeare, unsurprisingly, crops up a lot in this book. He hardly needs my advocacy, but his misbegotten work – so offensive to purists with its miscegenated mishmash of high and low culture, spliced genres and jerry-built structures – reveals that great plays amount to more than formal obedience. *Hamlet*, the keystone of his achievement, epitomises Shakespeare's inherently disobedient approach to convention. Leaving aside debates about editorship, the play is in theory too long, too diffuse, too slow, too open to subplots, too confused in genre. Judged in that light, it's hard to disagree with T.S. Eliot's famous verdict on the play that it was a failure, 'full of some stuff that the writer could not drag to light, contemplate, or manipulate into art'. But this is the paradox of *Hamlet*'s greatness. It shouldn't work, but it remains far more alive than many a play that obeys all the rules.

Hamlet's felicitous failings epitomise how playwriting, like theatre, is a paradoxical craft, conservative yet radical, backward- and forward-looking at once. Whilst it's almost possible to imagine a perfect poem or musical performance, applying the notion of perfection to a theatrical performance feels misplaced. Plays, in their rough-hewnness, encode that in advance. Edwardian theatrical polymath Edward Gordon Craig's doomed aspiration, expressed in his book *The Art of the Theatre*, to forge theatrical perfection by replacing the live, flawed body of the actor with puppets, only serves to confirm the fact that attempts to tidy up the craft risk killing off theatre's core appeal. A perfectly formed play would be as sterile and repellent as a perfect human community. This book focuses on particular plays that create their own local, stubborn and idiosyncratic norms. What they reveal can't easily be imported elsewhere – but the attempt to pin down how they appear to live might make emulating their example a little easier.

For there are continuities, conventions and trade secrets that flash out of plays as different as *Twelfth Night* and *Cleansed*, *Henry V* and *Christie in Love*, *Blood Wedding* and *Old Times*, arising from the constant yet ever-changing nature of theatre itself. The struggle to express inner life in outer action and word, the battle with the limits of the stage space, the wrestling with the raw material of time, yields family resemblances in plays from vastly different times and places. The hope I have in writing this book is that teasing out such affinities might contribute to the craft in the manner that *An Actor Prepares* and *Towards a Poor Theatre* have reconfigured the craft of acting – opening up possibilities rather than closing them down.

My impetus to write about playwriting came from two sources. Clarifying the first involves making a confession: I live a double life of teaching playwriting at the same time as writing plays – and, even more heretically, I find that a *productive* experience. Running the MPhil(B) in Playwriting at the University of Birmingham, a course established by the playwright David Edgar in 1989, and on which I myself studied, involves me working with fellow playwrights on their plays, hearing from other writers, musing over the literature: it's a privileged position, but it's also surprisingly fruitful. To borrow a term from French theory, writing is always an intertextual act: the plays of our predecessors generate ones we've yet to dream up. Being saturated in the work of others can be overwhelming, humiliating even, but more often it's enabling. I recognise why certain playwrights delight in airily telling us that they are more interested in movies and extreme sports than theatre, but I honestly don't believe them. No one after Aeschylus wrote a play without seeing or reading another one. Surely, then, more exposure and deeper engagement will create work that is more alive to the possibilities of the form.

Secondly, in that pedagogic role, I often find myself dismayed at the thin literature on playwriting, peering across enviously at writing on poetry and the novel by practitioners of both forms. Playwriting books are polarised between, on the one hand, high theory proclaiming the death of tragedy and the advent of post-dramatic theatre, and, on the other, guides that reduce narrative to diagrams and pronounce solemnly that 'drama is conflict'. Despite a raft of works on all the minutiae of the history of theatre or performance theory, playwriting, unless turned into something called 'radical dramaturgy', barely gets a look-in, except as a department of literary criticism.

One of the reasons for this lack is that playwrights rightly shun the systematic. David Edgar, mentioned above, is one of the very few who balances a knack for forensic clarity and creative openness, and his *How Plays Work* appeared during the writing of this book, definitively breaking that silence. But Edgar's the exception rather than the rule; most playwrights are reluctant to hold forth on the tricks of the trade. There's great wisdom to be gleaned from the fragments out there – Pinter in a forthcoming mood, Mamet's bilious accounts of his craft, Hare's scattered reflections, and more sustained works such as Ayckbourn's witty primer. And you can read Ibsen's notebooks from the time he was writing *Hedda Gabler* or eavesdrop on Chekhov's correspondence with Stanislavsky. Yet after two thousand years it's hardly a crowded field. Were I a poet I could read sustained essays of reflection and prescription by Milton, Coleridge, Keats, Yeats, Eliot, Pound, Heaney, Muldoon *et al*; were I novelist I could turn to the thoughts of Tolstoy, Eliot, Hardy, Woolf, Atwood, Kundera, to name but a few. Playwrights, it seems, are too busy fielding calls from agents, writing treatments and attending rehearsals and first nights to waste ink on why or how they do what they do. It's indicative that Brecht's great theoretical essays were written while he was in exile and debarred from the stage; that Shaw's prologues often headed up plays that failed to find a stage.

But it's not just that playwrights are busy. This resistance to reflection is also due to the crippling myth of the 'natural playwright', a kind of idiot savant that haunts the profession. The natural playwright doesn't need to read or think much about what they do because their plays ooze out of them effortlessly like sweat from a pore. What truth there is in such a caricature lies perhaps in the real fear that thinking too much will harm one's gift, that in naming the sources and secrets of the craft, writers might simply scare them off.

Such sources and secrets have often been expressed through ideas of visitation. In the Renaissance period, scholars used the notion of the 'vatic' to account for the act of inspiration – the writer seen as a mere vessel for a rage of invention, a poetic fury, entering them from outside. The figure of the muse, often portrayed as an ethereal lover, a nocturnal visitor who'd shrivel if exposed to daylight, personifies this idea. Henry Fielding's 1736 play *Eurydice Hiss'd* offers a vivid account of the relationship between an author and his muse. His writer, Pillage (a fictional self-portrait), laments that he has corrupted the muse's gifts by following money rather than her whims. Their once-respectful love has been reduced to a coercive transaction, and Pillage wails in vain, 'Come to my arms thou masterpiece of nature.' For Fielding, she (and after Hesiod, muses generally are female) is an embodiment of integrity, the unwilled and free workings of creativity. But above all, she's something 'natural', not part of the daylight world, an inhabitant of Eliot's 'dark embryo'.

Given this anxiety, it's perhaps no accident that some of the greatest playwrights of our time remain tight-lipped on their creative process. Caryl Churchill is notoriously gnomic about it; Harold Pinter, despite the occasional shirt-sleeve moment, generally nursed his mysteries. And certainly reflection can interrupt creation to disastrous effect, as if one were to start pondering the mechanics of the four-stroke engine whilst in the fast lane of the M11. How plays get written is indeed a profound mystery and this book would not dare to try to pronounce on any of those intensely unwilled and private matters.

But there are phases to the act of playwriting. The muse, if she exists, governs the dangerous, breach birth of the first draft, when the play emerges gory, unruly and untamed. It's a rare playwright who delivers that child ready to walk and speak; only with secondary, revisory work does that inchoate creature develop into something that is expressive to an audience rather than a private spasm. Left to its own devices, the dark embryo tends to yield up work that is, well, obscure and embryonic.

At this point, reflection can and does function. If you doubt it, look at the workings of modern theatres; this book is no manifesto for the burgeoning culture of the literary manager, but it would be perverse to argue that dialogue with a theatre is not an essential phase in the nurturing of private dreams into public art. Even that most theatrically untamed of writers, Georg Büchner, had several passes at *Woyzeck* – a process of revision cut tragically short by his death – and there is abundant scholarship tracking the skilful and wilful rewriting of *King Lear* and *Hamlet*.

Of course, playwriting occurs effectively enough without the crutch of theory or textbooks. But that's not to say that playwrights haven't hungrily devoured what wisdom they can from the scattered insights acquired on the job. Like many crafts, playwriting was, for its first two millennia, orally transmitted and preserved its trade secrets. But with the expansion of new writing for the theatre in the post-war era, it found a home in Britain and the USA in the academy too. I've mentioned David Edgar before, and much of the thinking that underlies this book I absorbed during my time on his seminal course. In many respects, before Edgar started to theorise about playwriting there wasn't anything much to talk about but Aristotle. And now in Edgar's long-awaited book, that thinking is laid out with crystalline lucidity.

But the courage Edgar gives us should enable a greater diversity of approach. Whilst it would be odd if this book did not chime with his in many respects, it's important to declare where it diverges too. Edgar's analysis, like his plays, is notable for its supreme intellectual confidence; a confidence earned from a life at the forefront of the craft and a career of political skirmishing; a confidence that is typical of Edgar's generation of baby-boomer leftist playwrights – Hare, Brenton, Barker and so on. Like all writers who have passed through the fire of Marxist polemic, Edgar is a seductive categoriser. The hard-won certainties about plays that inform his book are embodied in the promise of its title, *How Plays Work*. Edgar certainly delivers on that promise; but my caveat with his approach derives from the notion that plays 'work', with its implicit suggestion of something mechanistic about a play's inner being, something reducible to will-power alone. Whilst it's a subtle demurral, it goes a long way towards explaining why this book is as it is.

In place of Edgar's confident formalism, I offer here a tentative ecology of playwriting. Plays, like any ecosystem, consist of elements with their own separate integrity, which assemble to create effects beyond that separateness. Indeed, the potency of playwriting conventions derives from their interdependence. At the risk of sounding like David Bellamy, that ecological metaphor can be extended further. A play, like a wood, is an event in time rather than a fixed entity, dying and reforming through the years and seasons as it moves in and out of the repertoire. The ontological status of a play is problematic – which is a pretentious way of saying that a play exists somewhere between the page and the stage, that it is the sum total of all the versions that exist of it in time. Your *Mother Courage*, my *Mother Courage* and Brecht's *Mother Courage* are all real and all quite different, and the printed text doesn't necessarily adjudicate between them. In a sense, an unperformed play doesn't in fact exist, or at least remains in a state of latency.

Plays are like the Möbius strip, their separate components twisted into one continuous plane – time, space, language, character, symbol, seamlessly folded in on one another. Whilst those conventions can all be analysed independently of each other, and they often surface for the writer at different moments, in performance they are experienced as inseparably fused. Indeed if they don't, the play's likely to feel under-cooked, a recipe rather than a meal.

Plays resemble vital, natural organisms in another way. Their elements remain latent within them like the codes locked in DNA, able to form life whenever circumstances are favourable. We can all think of plays which disappear for gen-erations, appear thoroughly dead, only to emerge on the stage again revivified and new minted – *Troilus and Cressida* after World War II, *Hecuba* during the Iraq War. The playtext on the shelf or in the drawer is as dormant as a seed awaiting contact with the soil in order to erupt into existence; plays likewise carry within them stores of potential energy that combust on contact with an actor and an audience.

Such 'flowery' metaphors refer back to a Romantic concep-tion of the work of art as an organic entity, outlined by critics such as Coleridge. At worst that tradition has an obscurantist tenor, its cult of mystery serving as a way of keeping the unini-tiated reader and would-be writer out. But applying natural metaphors to human artefacts has the great virtue of respect-ing their complexity as something not quite reducible to their contrivances. The intent of the playwright is not dissimilar to the project of Mary Shelley's Victor Frankenstein – to create life out of an assemblage of elements. And in the end theatre is a live medium, about bodies, sweat and feeling, even if it is informed by ideas and reason. How a thing composed of words manages to carry within it the currents of energy that generate that impression of life is what I want to explore in these pages.

This emphasis goes some way towards accounting for the limited range of reference that follows. I draw my examples from a small selection of plays; partly, of course, as a reflection of my own narrow tastes, as taste cannot be legislated for. Yet the writers and plays represented here share a sense that life is a complex, mysterious affair, that human existence can only be understood with reference to a wider social landscape that is as active as the plays' protagonists. The reason I keep returning to certain plays – *Top Girls*, *The Cherry Orchard*,

Hamlet, Woyzeck, Translations, Old Times, Edmond, Miss Julie, The Wild Duck, The Oresteia, The Alchemist, Saved, Lear – and certain playwrights – Mamet, Churchill, Chekhov, Ibsen, Pinter, Aeschylus, Friel, Bond, Büchner – is not that I want to emulate F.R. Leavis's *The Great Tradition* and whittle all literature down to a handful of books, but rather that these plays have worked their way inside me, have made possible my very capacity to comprehend what theatre, and life, might be. Indeed, these plays have come to seem to me as complex and inexhaustible as people, and just as capricious and secretive in their workings. As in Erich Auerbach's *Mimesis*, his essential analysis of Western literature written in wartime Alexandria with an exile's library, or the brutally brief literary lineage outlined in Ezra Pound's *An ABC of Reading*, the repertoire of plays drawn on in this book offers a portable embodiment of two millennia of Western playwriting.

Equally, these works, when I re-encounter them, always carry a little piece of me within them: taking my first English class to see Max Stafford-Clark's revival of *Top Girls* in 1991; directing *The Cherry Orchard* in a scruffy hut in a rural comprehensive school; reading *Woyzeck* and, like Elias Canetti, finding myself almost blushing at its power; cycling to Stratford-upon-Avon to watch *Hamlet* and returning to a ridge tent. The plays in this book are still playing in rep within my mind, enabling me to recognise myself in the characters they harbour, reflecting back my life in the situations they enact, my own rhythms and voice in their languages.

So this book then is an attempt to talk to plays, to sound them out as with sonar.

To do that, it falls into three sections which, not entirely facetiously, I have called Acts. The first considers the workings of the key structuring decisions that give shape to plays in form, time and space. The second investigates the inhabitants and practices of those worlds – characters, language, images – and considers how emotion is encoded in all these elements. The third considers who playwrights are, where they stand in the theatre map, and what sorts of knowledge plays contain and playwrights possess.

Act One

Deep Structures

Chapter One
Changing Scenes

When Freud wanted to describe the origins of trauma, he spoke of 'the primal scene'. When a private tussle blows up in a public place we speak of 'making a scene'. Criminals return to the 'scene of the crime'. The concept of the scene has crossed over from theatre and shaped our deep structural sense of time and space. At a fundamental level, scenes correspond to the rhythm of lived experience. For life, like drama, is experienced as a sequence of time-limited, place-specific, purposeful scenes.

Think of an ordinary day: the fraught family breakfast with latecomers, offstage radio and the ticking clock of imminent appointments. The snatched encounter in the newsagent which suddenly expands as the retailer reveals some fragment of gossip that takes the moment beyond ritual. The idle chatter of commuters at the local train station. The drama of twenty minutes with a line manager or breaking bad news to a patient. The hectic badinage in the pub after hours. The tired pillow talk that precedes sleep.

Each event somehow finds its end, often through an exit or an entry, through some offstage imperative or onstage revelation. The moment passes, the business is dispatched, the choice is made, the Rubicon is crossed. Playwriting does not invent scenes, but rather it refines them into something more telling, more heightened, more moving – and more irreversible – than most of the scenes through which we live. And each scene in a play, like each cell in a body, is an embodiment of that play as a whole.

Consider the first scene of *Hamlet*. It is populated by marginal figures we'll meet only once again, namely Barnardo,

Francisco and Marcellus, alongside more crucial figures such as Horatio and of course the mute Ghost. Yet its first line is a question about identity which will reverberate throughout the entire play:

BARNARDO. Who's there?

FRANCISCO. Nay answer me. Stand and unfold yourself.

BARNARDO. Long live the king!

FRANCISCO. Barnardo?

BARNARDO. He.

FRANCISCO. You come most carefully upon your hour.

This confused encounter on the battlements before dawn, pregnant with false starts and curious rhythms, offers a model for the play to come, with its fitful progress, its lurchings from doubt to impulsive response. Even the fact that it is the guard, Francisco, who is challenged by his relief, Barnardo, proves a foretaste of the strange reversals and acts of usurpation that characterise the world of the play. Everything here suggests transition (the changing of the guard, the passage from night into day), and we are immediately attuned to the sense of dislocation that dominates the play.

These opening lines are so dense with meaning and action that they could almost amount to a scene in themselves – so why don't they? What exactly are the basic requirements of a scene? In theatrical terms the smallest unit of action is a line or gesture, here manifest in Barnardo's show-stopping challenge: 'Who's there?' The unravelling of that initial gesture reveals a larger unit of action, a beat, which persists up until 'You come most carefully...' where the scene's initial business is laid to rest. Directors often establish a further wordless beat before Barnardo's lunge and Francisco's riposte (not least out of kindness to Francisco, for this is pretty much the end of his night). Such beats stand midway in prominence and duration between a gesture ('Who's there?') and a scene; but why is it only a beat and not in fact a scene? Once the sentinels have cemented their mutual allegiance, another beat becomes evident in the moment of rest that ensues. The pair lament the lot of the nightwatchman ('For this relief much thanks'), assert comradeship and exchange facts, before the next crisis and beat, marked by the arrival of Marcellus and Horatio. Perhaps this next, longer beat is an unmarked scene? It isn't either, and the reason why is telling: nothing substantive happens within the beat; or rather, nothing changes. The beats at the start of the scene represent local problems which are granted local solutions (e.g. 'Who are you?' – 'I am your relief'). For a scene to emerge, larger, profounder and less soluble problems and changes need to occur.

Beats and gestures are unscientific terms, implicit in the action rather than defined in the form of a play. It's only at the level of the scene that we find a convention marked and generally understood. So is a scene simply a break in the text on the page? Clearly this is something that is inflected by genre and theatrical form. Gallic dramaturgical tradition tends towards long, unfolding acts broken down into so-called 'French scenes' that mark the entry or exit of a character; according to that convention two scenes would be demarcated on *Hamlet*'s first page. But in English dramaturgy that model is rarely observed and a scene can be as long as an act or as short as a gesture. Here in *Hamlet*'s opening, as with the phrase 'the scene is set', the determining element is not character presence, but a combination of place and time: from midnight (''Tis now struck twelve') until an accelerated dawn ('But look, the morn in russet mantle clad / Walks o'er the dew of yon high eastward hill'), up on the battlements. To that extent the scene still holds a kinship to its etymological origin in *skene*, which in Greek theatre alluded to the area above the orchestra or dancing place where the actions of protagonist and antagonist might take place.

Yet whether scenes begin and end with a coming and going, or a shift in time and space, something governs those transitions. For scenes, at bottom, are a form of action and an instance of change, even if that change is barely visible on the surface. Change is in itself an elusive term, but representing it is central to the art of playwriting. Even in Beckett's works, which seem stubbornly changeless, the very quality of Vladimir and Estragon's unrequited hope in *Waiting for Godot* or Winnie's desperate optimism in *Happy Days* is transformed by the intractable world they inhabit – the leaf falls from the tree in *Godot*, the mound grows higher in *Happy Days*. The nature of the change might lie in the circumstances, but more often, and even then, it's in the transformation of the characters; in Beckett, simply by seeing the play out, those characters acquire a kind of heroic status.

It's worth considering what is substituted for conventional scenes in works that have been characterised as 'post-dramatic'. In Sarah Kane's *Cleansed* or the later plays of Martin Crimp, who dubs his scenes 'scenarios', the action often has a suspended, imagistic quality; but time, and therefore change, is still at work. The overture of voices on an answerphone at the opening of Crimp's *Attempts on her Life* may seem to be merely fragments of text with no transformative quality, but hearing those voices seeking answers from the absent 'Anne', and finding none, provokes in us the gathering dread that all unanswered questions generate. Even if no one in the text changes, the audience is transformed.

Or think of the scene in *Cleansed* where the gruesome Tinker, head of a vaguely defined hybrid of university and concentration camp, forces Robin, one of his hapless inmates, to eat an entire box of chocolates. The stage directions are eloquently terse:

> ROBIN *eats the chocolate, choking on his tears.*
>
> *When he has eaten it,* TINKER *tosses him another.*
>
> ROBIN *eats it, sobbing.*
>
> TINKER *throws him another.*
>
> ROBIN *eats it.*
>
> TINKER *throws him another.*
>
> ROBIN *eats it.*
>
> TINKER *throws him another.*
>
> ROBIN *eats it.*
>
> [The sequence is repeated five more times.]
>
> TINKER *tosses him the last chocolate.*
>
> ROBIN *retches. Then eats the chocolate.*

What we seem to be watching is simply cruel repetition without change; but as the action unfolds in time, it shifts beyond cruelty into a mechanistic ritual that supersedes the torturer's wishes – Robin, mouth full of Milk Tray, acquires a curious power through enduring his torment, even as he soils himself in the process.

There are several layers of change apparent in *Hamlet's* opening scene – most obviously the changing of the guard – but the central shift lies in the changing of Horatio's mind. He arrives sceptical about the visitation of the Ghost (as Marcellus says, 'Horatio says 'tis but our fantasy'), his demeanour bespeaking his, and perhaps our, doubts (''Tush, tush, 'twill not appear'). But then occurs the inciting event of the scene, and indeed of the play – '*Enter* GHOST'. Horatio's transformation is instant, as Barnardo notes: 'How now Horatio? you tremble and look pale'. The overall story situation has not changed – the Ghost has walked and been witnessed before – but the transformation of Horatio underlines the true meaning of that event and nudges us towards the momentous events that await us – his new-found conviction leads him to connect this visitation to wider Danish turmoil ('This bodes some strange eruption to our state'). In fact, the Ghost appears a second time, and with its second manifestation we are in no doubt that this scene's shifts prefigure wider convulsions, and a task is established for the scenes to come (Horatio: 'Let us impart what we have seen tonight / Unto young Hamlet...'). Equally, that second haunting, which catches us out because the scene's business seems to have been done, is an example of Shakespeare's calculated irregularity – the scene exceeds its function, and appears more vivid as a consequence.

Creating conditions that provoke change is central to generating energy and momentum in plays. In a sense, a scene is a situation on the brink of becoming another one, a turning or tipping point; the severity of the resistance to that change determines its duration. So shocking is the presence of the Ghost that Horatio changes in an instant and the guards achieve their objective; it's the quickest shift this play will offer us.

So something necessitates the arrivals and the exits or propels us forward in time or elsewhere in space, and that something takes place in the scene and determines its length. After the writings of Stanislavsky, this something is increasingly identified as a form of action, and the subdivisions of that action called 'units of action'. And that action is usually a kind of transaction between the characters which advances or impedes their pursuit of a given objective. In the unfolding of those clashing objectives, the scene is a skirmish, the act a battle and the play is the war.

Put like this, the scene seems all too easy to fashion; surely it's just a matter of the dramatist mapping out their scenes, nestling them within acts and hoping it all combines into a play. And there are very good plays that appear to be built entirely on that principle, centring on a figure with an unbrookable will, who meets obstacles of increasing magnitude and dazzles us with their capacity to outface them. Such plays (think of *Richard III*) offer us a representation of their protagonist's life philosophy in their scenic DNA. The majority of *Richard III*'s scenes begin with Gloucester outlining his improbable objectives and daring us to doubt he'll achieve them – and sure enough, until the concluding battle scene, rivals get dispatched, hostile women are seduced and power is steadily acquired. The result is a purity but monotony of tone, largely because, whilst the situations in the play may change, the characters don't. Compare the superficially similar *Macbeth* for a much more offbeat and wrong-footing formulation of the same structure of action. Here all shifts in Macbeth's circumstances yield profound character transformations. And how very different again is *Hamlet*, where so often the objective is obscure to the protagonist himself – even in the first, simple scene, we wait about five minutes for its narrative purpose to be revealed. Indeed, until the end of Act One, when Hamlet finally meets the Ghost, the central objective of the play is deferred, and even then rendered problematic – finding an objective is itself the objective of the opening forty minutes.

Three Types of Scene

For a scene to remain a scene rather than a short play, it must yield something partial and unresolved, opening a door onto what follows as much as closing it on what's transpired. The most satisfying scenes create local transformations that detonate ever-larger movements beyond them. The duration, complexity and focus of any scene tell us an enormous amount about the nature of the story told.

To illustrate this, consider three sorts of scenes in three different plays by David Mamet. Mamet's ear for the boundaries and power of scenes is hard to rival in modern theatre. In his plays, a scene is like a blow to the face, a landscape revealed by lightning. Yet the three plays I want to look at – *Edmond* (1982), *Glengarry Glen Ross* (1983) and *Oleanna* (1992) – offer radically different takes on the nature of the scene, which in turn reveal some useful principles for all scenes.

Edmond is a brief, punky parable about a walk on the wild side, in which the eponymous yet rather generalised central male character abandons his tame middle-class world for the mean streets of an unnamed city, clearly New York in the days before Rudy Giuliani. His mid-life quest degenerates into a panorama of racism, exploitation and crime, to which he in turn ultimately succumbs – thus he tries to engage the services of a prostitute, he meets a racist in a bar, he buys a knife, he picks up a waitress, he attempts to connect with her and ends up killing her, he goes to prison. To enact the disjointedness of his experiences at the level of structure, Mamet limits the duration of each scene, with one exception, to no more than five minutes. Each scene features Edmond with a new or occasionally returning character. Each scene takes place in a new setting. And, until the extended scene with a waitress he picks up, each scene centres on a commercial or financial transaction between strangers.

The second scene, 'At Home' – Mamet gives each one a pithy title – is typical of the whole. It depicts Edmond's break-up with his wife and embarkation on a quest for the fulfilment that eludes him in everyday life. It might be possible to argue that Edmond enters the scene with a buried objective to begin this process of disentangling himself from all connection with that life – yet there's little evidence of anything except dull acquiescence:

> EDMOND *and his* WIFE *are sitting in the living room. A pause.*
>
> WIFE. The girl broke the lamp. (*Pause.*)
>
> EDMOND. Which lamp?
>
> WIFE. The antique lamp.
>
> EDMOND. In my room?
>
> WIFE. Yes. (*Pause.*)
>
> EDMOND. Huh.
>
> WIFE. That lamp costs over two hundred and twenty dollars.
>
> EDMOND (*pause*). Maybe we can get it fixed.
>
> WIFE. We're never going to get it fixed.
>   I think that's the *point*...
>   I think that's why she did it.
>
> EDMOND. Yes. Alright – I'm going.
>
>   *Pause. He gets up and starts out of the room.*
>
> WIFE. Will you bring me back some cigarettes?
>
> EDMOND. I'm not coming back.

That's it – the scene continues, but another type of play has begun to emerge. Admittedly, in the previous, cryptic, prologue-like scene, Edmond meets a fortune-teller whose diagnosis ('you are unsure what your place is') seems to pinpoint his malaise. But despite this, 'At Home' opens with a sustained image of inaction. The couple are seated, have presumably been seated for some time and might continue to remain there; they're marooned in a beat not unlike the moment before the Ghost arrives. And for ten lines or so Edmond is still in habitual, browbeaten mode, offering dull responses to his wife. Her lament about the lamp seems to be the catalyst to the disproportionate reaction that ensues, perhaps because for Edmond it is all too typical of marital life. And there's a real chance in the scene that the action might go no further than his feeble rejoinder of, 'Maybe we can get it fixed'. But then the volcano erupts – Edmond gets out of his chair.

Any director will attest to how difficult it is getting actors out of chairs, especially comfortable ones. But the energy of that gesture takes us instantly into a much more dangerous, unpredictable type of play.

In another writer's hands (or in another Mamet play such as *The Cryptogram*) this scene might have stood for the entire play. After all, we are invited into a life about to be abandoned – should we not see its charms in the rear-view mirror, the temptations to abide there? These would in that case be the psychological obstacles in the scene to Edmond's objective. Yet Mamet's intentions are otherwise. His characters here inhabit a quasi-behaviourist universe where physical actions precede intentions, even create them; at a midpoint in the scene, which seemed set up to outline the dull, quotidian nature of Edmond's world, he turns on his wife and subjects her to a litany of abuse. The velocity of this is almost comic ('you don't interest me spiritually or sexually'); the reaction equally ferocious ('Why didn't you leave *then*, you stupid *shit!!*'). From a scene that seemed to express inaction to one of almost melodramatic intensity, we are granted almost no transition time. The impact and heightening that ensues is almost elemental or expressionist; indeed the tempo of the play is reminiscent of a morality play such as *Everyman* in the suddenness with which both plays' everyday worlds open up to admit a type of hell.

So there is no doubting the presence of change in the scene; what's alarming is Mamet's refusal to indicate its cause. In its shocking theatricality, the scene shares an aesthetic with some of the most striking plays of modern times (Mark Ravenhill's 1996 play *Shopping and Fucking* obeys a comparable logic). The scenes in *Edmond* (which, given its ferocity, is mercifully short) simply observe Edmond's progress at its most intensely inhabited moments, with distractions pared away and other characters there simply to define him. His encounters are rendered with the barest of preliminaries, as we get to the core sexual or racial conflicts that lie barely concealed in urban life. But critical to this brevity is the mapping of power in the play. For Edmond's nihilism makes him uniquely powerful, and drives each interaction forward. Given that, after this scene, his interactions are almost exclusively with strangers, his refusal to accept small talk, the proprieties of interaction or courtesy, grants each scene a stark dynamic: that of his will versus an often stunned or comparably aggressive obstacle. The play moves fast because Edmond is renouncing all social restraint. This is a world without subtext and where people are dispensable to each other.

Compare these hard sketches of scenes – gestural, as rapid as a blink – to the much more sustained ones in *Glengarry Glen Ross*, which stages the bitter internecine conflicts of a bunch of real-estate salesmen in Reagan's America. The first half of the play is comprised of three scenes of about ten to fifteen minutes' duration, all duologues between men (although the last, between kingpin salesman Richard Roma and mute client James Lingk, is essentially a monologue). Why are they so sustained compared with the short, staccato scenes in *Edmond*?

The first two scenes – firstly between ageing salesman Levene and his immediate superior Williamson, secondly between fellow salesmen Moss and Aaronow – are between men in a shared professional context, albeit driven by a particularly high level of desperation. In each case, unlike in Edmond's world, these characters need each other; it isn't possible (although Williamson tries to do so) to dismiss or refute the needs of the partner in dialogue. In this world everyone is linked by the imperative of achieving sales, even if that link is extremely fragile and easily revoked. Yet at the same time, this is a competitive universe on the brink of criminality – intentions must remain hidden until they have to be disclosed. Indeed we are given at least two masterclasses in deception (Scenes Two and Three); yet whilst Lingk is a silent and largely unworthy opponent, and Aaronow destined to fulfil his promise as dupe, the objective of the initiating character must remain obscure until the last possible minute. Once the real intent of the scene is out, the objective achieved, there is no dying fall – the scenes come to an abrupt halt, as at the end of Scene Two, which crisply concludes with Moss's devastating pay-off to his victim Aaronow, 'Because you listened.'

The scene between Moss and Aaronow at first appears to be nothing more than two guys in a restaurant bitching about their clients:

> *A booth at the restaurant.* MOSS *and* AARONOW *seated. After the meal.*
>
> MOSS. Polacks and deadbeats.
>
> AARONOW....Polacks...
>
> MOSS. Deadbeats *all.*
>
> AARONOW....they hold on to their money...
>
> MOSS. All of 'em. They, *hey*: it happens to us all.
>
> AARONOW. Where am I going to work?
>
> MOSS. You have to cheer up, George, you aren't out yet.
>
> AARONOW. I'm not
>
> MOSS. You missed a fucking sale. Big deal. A deadbeat Polack.

The illusion of solidarity contrived here by Moss continues for some time as he stokes up Aaronow's resentment of their employer. Rather as in the opening of the 'At Home' scene in *Edmond*, we are in what looks like an entertaining but inert, objectiveless situation – it's after the meal, there seems no reason to hurry home, there's no obvious agenda. Then comes the first turning point, rather like the emergence of the Ghost in *Hamlet*, as Moss seems to fly a kite of rebellion: 'Someone should stand up and strike *back*'. This apparently vague intent is then narrowed down, with hilarious swiftness, to Moss's next proposition: 'Someone should rob the office'. A few beats later Aaronow comes out of his stupor and questions what is happening, only to be informed that he is now 'an accessory before the fact'; that the deal he didn't realise he was buying into has already degenerated into a rip-off. The impact of the scene lies precisely in the fact that we, like Aaronow, didn't realise that there was an objective being pursued – we didn't realise, in fact, that it was even a scene at all.

Here, as elsewhere in *Glengarry*, the scene's ostensible action is a smokescreen; its true action lies in the protagonist breaking down all possible resistance to their buried objective.

The third sort of scene in Mamet's work is apparent in *Oleanna*, which anatomises the disastrous attempt of liberal educationalist John to engage with the despair of his mediocre student Carol at her incapacity to thrive in Higher Education. To tell this story Mamet creates sustained encounters of about a forty-minute duration, which look rather more like acts than scenes. What, therefore, does it mean for a scene to swell to act length? In the great naturalist plays, short, episodic, free-standing scenes are avoided as they break the hold of real time and make the experience of the story fragmentary. Classic naturalist plays offer us instead an open field of time, where change seems to occur without any authorial manipulation. Yet even in these plays, as we shall see in the next chapter, their seemingly uninterrupted, symphonic acts carry within themselves numerous subdivisions and subplots. *Oleanna* might adopt that form, but as a two-hander its potential for orchestrating such internal changes is rather circumscribed.

Also, unlike the rich, detailed layering apparent in, for instance, the first act of Brian Friel's *Translations*, where the world onstage and off is densely populated and steadily unfolded, *Oleanna* shares with our previous Mamet plays a starkness of presentation (its setting a non-descript campus room) and a relentlessness of focus (bar the choric interruptions of the telephone). Yet again, on close scrutiny it's obvious why the short scenes of *Edmond*, or the longer yet equally pithy scenes of *Glengarry*, have expanded to ones that last up to forty minutes: this is a world hemmed in by tact, protocol and malfunctioning language, where saying even the simplest thing is immensely difficult. Whereas in the other plays Mamet has an unnamed yet monosyllabic need or a withheld yet ever-apparent objective driving the action, here Carol, the instigator of the scene, has a need so confused and inarticulate that it takes forty minutes to emerge, and even then will be entirely misunderstood.

This play, unlike *Glengarry*, does not take place in a 'world of men'. Mamet throughout his work presents interaction between men and women as largely doomed to failure; but his real target here is the increasingly hermetic world of the academy, and the stultifying codes of political correctness. The scene/act then becomes driven not by Carol but by John's initial attempts to remove Carol; and then his ultimate attempts to keep her in the room in order to convince her of the value of a liberal education. Yet Carol's intractable inarticulacy becomes his obstacle, stripping away his habitual stratagems and forcing him to achieve a new kind of didactic intensity – which will be his undoing.

> CAROL. I'm just trying, I'm just trying to...
>
> JOHN....no, it will not do.
>
> CAROL....what? What will... ?
>
> JOHN. No. I see, I see what you, it... (*He gestures to the papers.*) but your work...
>
> CAROL. I'm just: I sit in class I... (*She holds up her notebook.*) I take notes...
>
> JOHN (*simultaneously with 'notes'*). Yes. I understand. What I am trying to *tell* you is that some, some basic...

Much of the opening of the play consists of beats straining to become action; but the sheer dissonance of this dialogue of the deaf prevents change. The means the characters use to communicate with each other becomes a barrier to communication – language, here reduced to a wail of feedback. The opening ten minutes are an unbearable tease – through all the inarticulate flailing we sense a scene on the horizon, but have to endure Carol's hyperventilation and John's fractured authority chafing against each other. Compare this with 'At Home' from *Edmond*; had John been Edmond, the scene would have ended in seconds. In many respects the play works as a device to strip away John's layers of civility until he ends up kicking Carol under the desk. In terms of action alone the scenes in *Oleanna* really needn't be as long as an act – but the very fact that matter appropriate for a short scene plays out at such length exemplifies the friction Mamet is satirising.

In all these types of scenes there are common determinants of the duration of the scene:

The distribution of power

The more evenly distributed the balance of power, the harder it is to realise an objective, the more subtext comes into play, the longer the scene. Edmond's indifference to his wife's concerns permits a swift exit and so the scene is brief. Horatio, who is the object of the first scene, is of higher status than the guards, so he won't be persuaded of the Ghost's existence until he sees it for himself. The salesmen in *Glengarry* have apparently equal professional status, which masks real inequalities. And most complex of all is the kind of power Carol possesses over John, derived from his own self-image as a liberal who can educate anyone, as well as her status as a victim in a world of political correctness.

The clarity of the objective

In *Hamlet*, the objective – persuading Horatio of the Ghost's reality – is not complex, but for it to be achieved the Guards must abandon their usual protocols and – above all – the Ghost must put in an appearance. In *Edmond*, most of the scenes are driven by clear, localised objectives which often accord with their environment. In *Glengarry*, the objectives are more illicit and require greater degrees of collaboration of the antagonist in the scene. In *Oleanna*, the obscurity of the objective itself becomes the core of the scene.

The social texture of the situation

This obviously relates to the first point but the nature of the world dictates how easy it is to get things done. In *Hamlet*, the very confusions at the heart of Denmark's state hamper the action, as do martial protocols and the intimation that what is revealed might have potentially seditious implications. In *Edmond* the cheap, impersonal world of the city allows for fast, ugly yet realisable transactions. In *Glengarry* these transactions are more complicated and rely on psychological manipulation and exploitation – after all, here, unlike in *Edmond*, the protagonists are selling scams and schemes, which necessitates a degree of deviousness. In *Oleanna*, the sheer vexatiousness of a world in a state of chronic self-consciousness means that the simplest of gestures is almost impossible to achieve.

Equally, all scenes have a type of common, inner structure which mirrors the larger structure of the play. This again can be broken down:

Situation
The circumstances at the opening of the scene, which need to be deftly and swiftly evoked. In *Edmond*, 'the girl broke the lamp' takes us in one simple lament right into the heart of this world, this relationship, this malaise; or the anxious watch of Francisco, or indeed the apparently comradely meal shared by Moss and Aaronow; or John's attempt to leave his office and dispatch some personal business at the end of a working day.

Transformation
At some point that balance or pre-existing relationship will be placed under stress in the scene – by new knowledge, new objectives, new circumstances: the arrival of Horatio and then the Ghost; Edmond's sudden impulse to leave; Moss's scheme to rob the boss; Carol's desperate supplication. This will be the core concern of the scene.

Propulsion
Because a scene is not a play it does not achieve completion; even if the transformation promised is locally achieved, it cannot generate a complete equilibrium – change here generates new circumstances which necessitate further changes to come: Horatio's new-found conviction impels him to acquaint Hamlet with the Ghost; Edmond's departure generates questions about how he will fare with his new-found appetite for living; Aaronow's apparent acceptance of his implication in the crime commits him to participate in it; Carol's broken-off confession implies a new phase in her assault on John.

Scenes, then, are units of dramatic energy, the muscles that drive the play forward. In order to optimise their propulsion they need to be focused and populated in such a way as to serve the dynamic of the larger story. If the scene begins too early or too late, if it's populated by too many or too few or ill-judged characters, the impact on the play will be disastrous. Every scene, no matter how seemingly disposable, affects the play's trajectory. Imagine, for instance, that *Hamlet* didn't begin with the scene on the battlements: it's perfectly possible to begin the play at Scene Two, to go straight into the heart of Claudius's Court, thereby reaching Hamlet much sooner; Horatio still brings news of the Ghost to him at the end of that scene, so there's no apparent narrative loss. We don't, in truth, need Barnardo, Marcellus or Francisco, and we only just need Horatio. Yet a moment's contemplation reveals how the whole energy of the play would be fatally disrupted by such a cut. After Scene One, and the shock of the Ghost, we watch everything with a new vigilance; and after meeting those ill-treated, discontented watchmen and hearing rumours of the rottenness that might lie at the heart of Denmark, we are better placed to hear Hamlet's lament as more than self-pity, and we are more likely to distrust the smooth running of the Court.

In the playwright's choice of scenes lies their whole philosophy of life. For Mamet, the contested nature of every scene portrays life as a place of constant risk and conflict, marked by astonishing intensity. For Shakespeare, especially in *Hamlet*, every moment opens out into dizzying perspectives – from the personal to the metaphysical. Nothing marks out a playwright more than how they handle the scene, what they furnish it with. But the disposition and distribution of those scenes, the energy that jumps between them, is a larger question, and one that means we must now consider the act – for it is the act that turns the scene's pulse into the play's current of life.

Chapter Two
Shaping Acts

How many acts has your life contained so far? Act One is perhaps your childhood, climaxing with the loss of your virginity, the time your parents split up, or the move to a new country. Act Two is your first job, your university years, your fall from grace, your first lover – it might close with you waving your degree certificate, or perhaps being expelled through the revolving door of a large corporation, or even joining the rebel army in the borderlands. Act Three is the working through of the portents of the first two acts: the marriage doomed by the damage done to you in childhood; the job that slowly kills you; the struggle to gain or retain power. If you are lucky enough to get an Act Four it could bring the dissolution of everything or the restoration of everything, according to the vision of life you have acquired along the way.

When writers talk of how their plays eschew judgement, how they refuse to moralise, how they have moved beyond ethical consideration, they neglect to mention that the very act of shaping a story in time is an act of judgement. The act structure of a play determines where we begin and where we end, and within these moments the characters' fates are disclosed; life is revealed.

More pragmatically, carving out a structure in time through acts determines the sort of evening the audience will experience. As playwright Stephen Jeffreys has insightfully observed, the event structure of the evening is founded upon the act structure of the play – the presence or absence of the interval, for instance, transforms the nature of the event in time. Time and dramatic storytelling have a complicated but fundamental relationship, and this chapter is only partially about time. But underpinning that relationship is the audience's capacity to sit and watch, and it's a truism that most dramatic events find themselves responding to a basic human need to get up, move around, talk, go for a pee, a smoke, or a drink. As a consequence, the two hours' traffic of the stage proclaimed in the Prologue to *Romeo and Juliet* is the default setting for most plays, films, ballets, even, *pace* Wagner, operas. This in turn governs what sort of story can be told. As I write I am eagerly anticipating watching the box set of *The Wire*, Season One, which clocks in at 770 minutes of viewing time. Despite its apparently unfeasible length, I am reassured by the knowledge that American television series are conventionally broken down into hourly chunks, themselves punctuated by ad breaks, often conforming to four-act structure, each act closing with some hook or shock or shift. As it's on loan from the library and I have three weeks to watch it, I am tempted to binge; but should I really spend four hours a night watching something designed as intense bursts of one-hour consumption over a period of months? Would doing that cut across the grain of the leisurely, diffuse act structure television offers us, where the unfolding of the story sits alongside the episodic experience of our lives?

Such a profligate relationship to time is not given to playwrights or their audiences; with the exception of cycles of Mystery plays unfolding over a day, or Shakespeare's chronicle plays packaged as similar cycles, plays retain their ergonomic shape in time. After all, the audience members have turned up at the theatre and will go home at the end of the evening – how much time are they prepared to grant the playwright and how much of their time can the playwright assume? A parallel with novelistic storytelling is perhaps pertinent – the twelve hours of *Harry Potter and the Goblet of Fire* as read by Stephen Fry kept my family quiet during four long car journeys to Wales. But for all Fry's ingenuity, digesting a long book in four-hour stretches breaks the leisurely contract of narrative time as established in the novel. Bingeing on chapter after chapter induces a narrative nausea that the tactful act structures of plays seek to avoid.

Certain patterns and traditions in play structure, therefore, arise from the needs of the audience. These patterns are not legally binding, but if they're flouted the audience will need to sense strong mitigating circumstances. Why, after the interval, is the second half of the show usually shorter than the first? This is surely less about physical discomfort than the fact that we have done the narrative work and are now ready to glide along with the momentum of the play's pay-offs. Otherwise, why are there are so few acts that break the forty-five-minute barrier? Largely, I think, because humankind can only bear so much real time: we crave substantial change, a craving that cinema gratifies every minute. Then why do critical events in an act tend to occur about five minutes before its close? Because we need time to register the climax, feel ourselves to be within the spell of the narrative still and then to be taken out of it. Why are there rarely more than five acts in a play? Perhaps because the sixth or seventh acts are either too brief in themselves to earn the name of act, or are so long as to push the story out of theatre and into the domain of the novel. Finally, why does a one-act play not feel like a satisfactory entertainment for an entire evening? The recent vogue amongst playwrights for delivering plays of thirty to fifty minutes still provokes complaints at the box office about value for money. So if the play is short, it must compensate with an intensity that reverberates beyond the curtain call (as does, say, Caryl Churchill's *A Number* or debbie tucker green's *born bad*, *trade* or *random*).

The placing of events within the acts reveals the next set of considerations. How soon into the action should the first major event occur and how much time is necessary to prepare the audience for it? *Hamlet* again is instructive: were the Ghost to appear as the lights go up, a theatrical coup would be achieved for sure, but there would then be much breathless catch-up exposition (that was young Hamlet's father; we are in Denmark; you are Horatio, Hamlet's friend) dulling its impact, and the capital of the short-term effect would be squandered. Meeting Hamlet too soon would be a mistake – by withholding him for ten brave minutes, Shakespeare defers gratification wonderfully; and then, his entry into the play is on a cryptic aside ('a little more than kin, a little less than kind'). If his first soliloquy had preceded the Court scene with Claudius, the ticking bomb of his silence would not then have undermined the dazzling statecraft in the foreground. The act structure in any play balances the audience member's need for story, and their bodily needs.

Acts are the largest units of representation within the play, and give form to the great sweeps of thought that underlie the action. There's an excitement that accompanies the end of an act – the curtailment of the action, the lurch forward into an unknown future. The act break is an opportunity for the playwright to exploit surprise. One of the most breathtaking transitions in modern theatre occurs between Act Two and Act Three of Harley Granville Barker's *The Voysey Inheritance*, where we reel out of one great Edwardian family gathering at the foot of the titular paterfamilias in Act Two, only to enter another in Act Three where it becomes apparent that the father has died in the interim, and the gathered storm of his legacy of toxic debt is about to break over his progeny. That cataclysmic transition is as expressive as anything within the acts themselves. Similarly, in Barker's *Waste* the act structure advances us into a terrifying moral dilemma as Trebell, its independent MP protagonist, finds his casual sexual liaison with married woman Amy O'Connell plunging him into an increasingly excruciating predicament. As with *Voysey*, the shift from Act Two to Act Three is especially brutal: in the act-break mortality and disgrace intervene, with Amy dying at the hands of an abortionist. The double movement of Trebell's attempt to disestablish the Church of England and the breaking scandal of his moral lapse reach consummation as he is confronted by his political peers and ultimately driven to suicide.

Barker's deeply ethical structural sense operates not so much in the lines of the play as in the beating drum of the act structure, which declares that time will move forward, that consequences will work through. This is apparent in the placing of events within the acts; so much of the first act of *Waste* is concerned with political manoeuvring recounted to us by the politicians' wives, and Trebell's sexual dalliance with Amy occurs rather like an afterthought in the closing moments of the act. Yet this apparently marginal event, of which we see only a teasing glimpse, upstages all other plot elements as the acts grind forward. We are being led from the public to the private, from men to women, just as the acts take us more intimately into the circumstances of Trebell's life.

Novelists, of course, deploy the same effects: think of Virginia Woolf's luminous *To the Lighthouse* with its three-act structure – its Parts are devastating in their shape and effect, with 'Acts One and Two' depicting the Ramsay family at their Scottish retreat with and without the anchor of the life-affirming Mrs Ramsay, separated by the lyrical time-lapse effects of a kind of interval where we see the house without their tutelage. Likewise, Philip Roth's ferocious and theatrical late novels such as *American Pastoral* or *Sabbath's Theatre* manipulate time into passages of maximum energy and revelation, and reproduce the accelerations and decelerations of time which a good play should offer, as his protagonists hurtle towards death or confrontation.

Of course, some plays occur in unbroken time. In such plays the act structure may not be immediately apparent, but it is at work under the skin of the action and the dramatist's task is therefore that much harder, as we will see in our later discussion of Strindberg's *Miss Julie*.

If the shaping of experience into scenes is central to the craft of playwriting, the act structures within which these scenes sit reveal the playwright's deeper narrative powers. In this there is a kinship with the novelist, but perhaps more tellingly with the composer of a symphony. For behind all playwriting and composing, there is the same intuitive grasp of time management, of the power to potently select and assemble and orchestrate events, motifs or structures in time.

Acts are as various as theatre itself. The evolution of act structures through time is in some ways the evolution of the play and the stage – yet, as with evolution in the natural world, this has not been a process of one form displacing and replacing another, but of a steady sedimentation of formal possibilities. In marking out some of the major stepping stones in that evolution, many of the act structures I land on are eccentric – or even in some cases perverse. Yet in their aberrant quality they reveal what an act might be and the internal workings of other, less contentious plays.

Tragic Acts

The act as specified within the text itself comes late in the history of playwriting, not until Seneca's plays in the first century CE. Yet the idea of an act is implicit in plays from the outset of recorded drama. Admittedly, this is not immediately obvious when you look at the texts of Greek tragedy – most of the plays that survive offer us a purity and singularity of form that seems to contradict the notion of act divisions. *Oedipus Tyrannus* – Aristotle's great exemplar – appears to demonstrate a single unfolding action, uninterrupted and exquisitely organised, and few Greek tragedies have scene breaks let alone act breaks.

Yet look at their internal and external organisation and it becomes clear that Greek tragedies observe act-like divisions nonetheless. *Oedipus* is striated with choric interventions which announce the shifts and forward movements of its action; on four occasions, the Chorus turn to the audience and away from Oedipus and – given that those lines are couched in more organised verse and were probably accompanied in performance by dance and singing – they provide a kind of breathing space in the intensity of the narrative action and an elision in time. Indeed, in each of these cases Oedipus leaves the stage for most of the choric interruption. The break in form (from the intense world of the story organised around dialogue to the lyrical hymns and strophes of the Chorus) and in time (time out from the rapidly unfolding sequence of revelations in the story, and time for reflection enacted for the audience by the Chorus), offer a model for all subsequent act structures to follow.

Further structural divisions emerge from these apparently undivided plays when the circumstances of their first performances are considered. They were written to be staged in a festive context, often as part of a tetralogy of works: three tragedies and one satyr play. Frustratingly few of these complete tetralogies survive – so the dazzling close of Euripides' *Medea*, for instance, with its avenging infanticidal mother in triumph, aloft in her chariot, might well have been succeeded by a play that countered that shock. But one of the earliest trilogies of tragedies thankfully does survive: Aeschylus's *The Oresteia* possesses a structure which is a prototype for the three-act structure, each of its three plays equivalent to an act. Whilst the trilogy taken in one gulp exceeds the conventional two hours' traffic, it amounts to little more than four hours in theatrical time, and is entirely conceivable, even in our more impatient theatrical conditions, as a single theatrical work.

Thus in *Agamemnon* we have the brooding prehistory of the House of Atreus, with the return of the eponymous hero into the web of Clytemnestra's lair; its climax a brilliant 'first-act closer', a hair-raising image of crime in the ascendant as the murderous, vengeful wife and her complaisant lover Aegisthus revel over the corpse of the dead patriarch. The second play, *The Libation Bearers*, offers us the second act of this intractable family drama, with Orestes' return from exile and his wavering resolve to avenge his father stiffened by his unflinching sister Electra. The climactic slaughter of mother and lover which seems to be the answering response to the originating crime is in fact far more ambivalent in its ugliness (not least because we see more of it, whereas Clytemnestra's crime is withheld from us), and ushers in Act Three in *The Eumenides*, where the insatiably vengeful appetites of the Furies can only be assuaged by a trial presided over by Athena – thus liberating Orestes from his burden and founding a new form of citizen justice in the process.

The organisation of this trilogy reveals a great deal about the structural principles of acts. Firstly, a story of about thirty years' duration (from the origins of the Trojan War, the sacrifice of Iphigenia through to the final establishment of a new polity) is plotted into three elegant and intense moments in time and space. This is most purely achieved in the first play, which unfolds seamlessly within the one night of Agamemnon's homecoming; the second act offers another return, this time by Orestes to a marginal space beyond the palace, where the past is palpable in Agamemnon's grave and in the circular rituals of mourning enacted by Electra. Yet in the second play, the action breaks into two moments – the return of the son and then his arrival at the threshold of the palace where intentions must become action. Finally, in the last play the flight of Orestes necessitates another type of action, more diffuse in space and choric in the telling, guiding us away from the parochial blood feuds of the House of Atreus into wider questions of justice itself.

Structure here is meaning. Aeschylus's architectural conception of story is profoundly revealing, in some respects even more so than Sophocles' *Oedipus Tyrannus*, which crushes its family saga into a pressure-cooker plot of two hours' duration. Aeschylus shows how act structure is a form of thinking; his plays interact dialectically in a particularly pure fashion, long before Hegel's formulation of that notion:

Agamemnon

CORE ACTION – Clytemnestra revenges her dead daughter.

THESIS – In Clytemnestra's revenge on Agamemnon we see the past deform the present and the bottomless hatred that revenge unleashes on the world.

The Libation Bearers

CORE ACTION – Orestes avenges his dead father.

ANTITHESIS – In Orestes' consequent return and faltering crime we see the next generation attempt to rid itself of that maimed past; but the new slaughter only unleashes further horror.

The Eumenides

CORE ACTION – The Furies revenge Clytemnestra.

SYNTHESIS – In Athena's rigged trial we see a new form of justice expounded at one remove from the injured parties and thus the cycle of retribution is closed.

The Oresteia, with its wide-ranging focus and shifting conceptions of character and chorus, inaugurates the idea that a theatrical narrative can operate through idea and theme. Indeed it shows that each act might offer not only a new focus but also a different way of telling the story. This is discernible in the shifting nature of the Chorus in the three plays: in the first, they occupy the classic role of witnesses, as emasculated old men relegated to the margins of the story; in the second, they become aligned with a character and a project, as the handmaidens of Electra, and advocates thereby for revenge; in the third, as the Furies, they have become protagonists, with Orestes in passive reaction. By changing the Chorus's function, and indeed by adopting an increasingly supple theatrical style, progressively diffuse in time and place as the trilogy proceeds, Aeschylus reveals how acts are not merely units of time, they also modulate the way in which the story is told.

The Shakespearian Act

After the Greeks and Seneca, Shakespeare is surely the next great act innovator, extending further the notion of what an act might contribute to the telling of a story. His dexterousness with act structure is honed in his chronicle plays, where he was compelled to emplot a huge and confusing canvas of action into digestible narrative shape, both within individual plays and across sequences of them. The convention of the five-act structure he inherited from Seneca granted him a new fluency of narrative, as well as opportunities to deepen and make more complex the stories he told. Shakespeare's great skill at this is even more apparent when you compare his act structures with those of his most accomplished contemporary, Christopher Marlowe. *Doctor Faustus*, whilst almost certainly a work of collaboration, has a very variable dramatic energy and focus, and only really attains genuine tragic intensity in the opening and concluding acts, where time is suddenly urgent and condensed, and the action, which elsewhere is digressive, is configured into a deadly duologue. Similarly, *Edward II* is notably repetitive and monotonous structurally; its final swerve into continuous time and action, as Edward is immured in Berkeley Castle, only emphasises the loose episodic quality of what precedes it. Yet this structure of four episodic acts followed by a devastating closing confrontation, which Marlowe reuses throughout his work, is brilliantly reinvented by Shakespeare in *Richard II* and *Antony and Cleopatra*, to name but two instances.

The diversity of act structure in Shakespeare's plays defies description and is attributable to the dazzling generic diversity of his work. *Hamlet* reveals him at his most cunning and complex in this respect. With its five-act structure and revenge-genre trappings, the play draws on both Seneca and contemporary drama such as Kyd's *The Spanish Tragedy*. That structure is designed to serve the basic revenge story: a terrible wrong is done to the protagonist; that wrong in an unjust world meets with no punishment; the revenger takes the task upon himself; but the odds against him impel him to adopt a disguise, feigning madness before ultimately succumbing to it; with the end result a terrible massacre. *Hamlet* structurally complicates that model and inflates it into a much more suggestive and open-ended kind of story. Most of the acts have their climaxes subtly undermined, and the apparent logic of the act structure leads us into surprising and complex territory, not least because Shakespeare uses his two extra acts (if we take the three-act structure as the norm) to widen his narrative and generic repertoire. So *Hamlet* is at once the story of Hamlet's own internal transformations and also of Denmark's wider tribulations; indeed the character who keeps the play on the move is so often not its true protagonist, but the inhabitants of the simpler play it springs from – Claudius, Polonius and Laertes bear the narrative strain rather than the play's troublesome lead.

This muddying of expectations is clearly demonstrated by the close of Act One, which ends with Hamlet meeting with the Ghost – but the terrible testimony of Old Hamlet is then subverted by five further minutes of clowning and gallows humour concerning the under-stage Ghost's injunctions that Hamlet should swear his fellows to secrecy. In fact, other than resolutions to 'wipe away all trivial fond records' from his brain, Hamlet reaches the end of the act with only the rather vague project of adopting his 'antic disposition'. More importantly, that strict separation of genres and focus on the core moral question that occurs in Greek tragedy is replaced with unpredictable lurches into comedy and a questioning of the very matter of the play. The end of Act One, which had thus far been relatively obedient in its structure, confirms that we are in for a long and troubling night.

After this ambivalent climax, Act Two begins with Hamlet daringly withheld from us, his 'antic disposition' fraught with ambiguity. The arrival of the Players, whilst they will ultimately serve his purpose, deflects us further from the apparent project of the play. The act ends anticlimactically with Hamlet's soliloquy of eloquent self-loathing; indeed, without Claudius's counter-plot to sound his nephew out, the action would lose its frame of forward momentum altogether. Act Three is even more curiously shaped, initially switching back to Claudius and Polonius's project, yielding a soliloquy ('To be or not to be') which seems in its concerns to hark back to Hamlet's opening state of mind; all reference to the revenge plot he's actually in is absent. The closing impetus of Act Two seems forgotten: shouldn't the 'Mousetrap' follow hard on the heels of the resolution formed there instead of being delayed for a scene? The 'Murder of Gonzago' yields famously double-edged results, but with Hamlet's speech of true revenger savagery at the end of that scene ('Now I could drink hot blood'), we seem at last on the cusp of some punitive violence. These simple pleasures are rudely deferred again in the agonising scene of Claudius's soliloquy at prayer, which instead offers a (very late) confirmation of his actual guilt, undercut by his all too human remorse, which makes Hamlet's murderous reflections seem coarse. Then we have the most misshapen scene in the play, the closet scene, where the timing of Polonius's death – a third of the way through – is bizarrely nonchalant, and the focus again veers from Hamlet's ostensible project into something much more psychotic. There can be few braver and more confusing act-closers than this one, with Hamlet 'lugging' the corpse of Polonius and intoning, 'Good night, mother'.

If *Hamlet*'s act structure so far has tinkered with our expectations, it then goes haywire. Act Four is a mess, enacting Denmark's own disintegration. The scenes drastically shorten, held together only by Claudius's self-serving desire to banish Hamlet. The Prince's fitful entries and exits resemble nothing other than the manic infantilism of the Marx Brothers; the death of Ophelia crashes into the midst of this, pulling focus; then Elsinore is abandoned with filmic verve as Hamlet witnesses the progress of Fortinbras's troops and returns to the self-abnegation of his earlier soliloquies. Even bolder is the break in time here, and the return in Act Five to the dilatory graveyard scene that seems indifferent to the play in which it is placed. The onus is on Laertes to bring us back to the revenge plot, and even then the final reckoning is cruelly deferred by that ultimate dramaturgical solecism, the late-arriving, superfluous character of Osric.

    Hamlet, then, strikingly reveals how act structure can guide, even trick the audience into an ever-deepening experience of moral profundity, through both gratifying and disappointing their expectations. On paper, the play offers everything we want of an evening of blood and thunder – ghosts appear, crimes are revealed, madness is feigned, politickers killed, and we end with the thrill of a duel. But Shakespeare's positioning of all these events reneges on the gratification they should offer. The Ghost appears, but then becomes a comic stage effect; when he reappears he is presented as a hallucination; the crime is revealed, but in such an equivocal fashion that recourse against it can't be sought, while the truth of the matter is not confirmed for the audience until Act Three, and indeed never fully for Hamlet; the 'antic disposition' is proposed, but in practice its functioning is rarely clear and overlaps all too painfully with Hamlet's own internal turbulence; yes, Polonius is killed, but his death feels random and disproportionate and triggers the entirely secondary death of Ophelia; we get our duel, but it's rigged, it features the wrong combatants and it leads to an inelegant slaughter which hardly delivers what the audience thought they wanted.

    This list of wilful refusals to gratify us can in fact be turned on its head – for each of these reversals pushes us deeper into a new kind of drama of emotional complexity, a new kind of realism which questions the certainties of genre. We don't get what we expect, but the act structure makes us experience that, not as a lack, but rather as a shift into another level of story – what we get is life, vivid, irregular and morally confused.

Shakespeare's innovative sense of structure as meaning is equally evident in *Antony and Cleopatra*, which pushes to the limit how much contradictory reality a play can gather together into one evening's matter. Famously switching deftly between the worlds of Rome and Egypt (thus enabling a raft of sixth-form essays to be written on that very subject), its structural triumph lies in the fluent unfolding of the double biographies of its characters, their ebbing fortunes mapped against each other with the precision of a spirit level:

ACT ONE – Antony's return to Rome on the death of Fulvia and imminent civil war; Cleopatra spurned.

ACT TWO – The threat of Pompey and formation of the triumvirate; Cleopatra's rage; Antony's marriage with Octavia; the truce with Pompey.

ACT THREE – The revocation of the truce with Pompey; Antony's rejection of Octavia and return to Egypt; the battle and rout at Actium.

ACT FOUR – Caesar in Egypt; the defection and suicide of Enobarbus; Antony's failed suicide and Cleopatra's mock death; Antony's death.

ACT FIVE – The tempting of Cleopatra and her refusal of Caesar; the final suicide of Cleopatra.

The acts are implicitly structured around the following elements:

Place – The first three acts manipulate fractured space; the final two represent the convergence of place and character – in a sense the play comes to Cleopatra, funnelling its energy into her Court.

Protagonist – This is a multi-protagonist play where subplot and main plot are seamlessly woven together. Thus the carrier of the story is changed from act to act, necessitating a complex act structure.

Chorus – Making coherent the complexity of the central triad of characters (Antony, Cleopatra, Caesar) are other marker characters – storytellers and messengers, most notably Enobarbus but also Dolabella, Charmian and the Soothsayer. Remarkably they too participate and are transformed by the core action.

What's fascinating about Shakespeare's adoption of a five-act structure is the way it transforms the inherent morality of the story he's telling. Whereas three acts suggests 'a thought in three parts' (after the title of Wallace Shawn's play), five acts builds into the story complexity and controlled diffuseness. In a sense the story tracks the movement away from and back to a determining desire, and indeed the plot's focus suggests the triumph of love over historical fact; Caesar may win, but his victory is as pyrrhic as Fortinbras's in *Hamlet*, in that his subjugation of Egypt is simply external and the promise of Cleopatra eludes him. Yet the five-act structure allows us to observe the conflicting forces in Antony's life torn between Rome and Egypt, and at the same time enables two, or even three, equally compelling character-driven plays – 'Antony' and 'Cleopatra' and 'Caesar' – to coexist. To pull this off, Shakespeare deploys genre with astonishing deftness:

ACT ONE, Comedy – The play begins in an Egypt of punning hedonism. In this world, the tragic news of Fulvia's death and the ominous disapproval of Rome make no impact; Cleopatra's reaction to that news ('Can Fulvia die?') could have been penned by Noël Coward.

ACT TWO, Roman Play – Cleopatra is now a side dish; we are in Rome and the foreground is dominated by the forging of the triumvirate of Lepidus, Antony and Octavius, the containment of Pompey's menace and the expedient marriage of Antony with Octavia; Cleopatra is more spoken of than seen.

ACT THREE, History Play – After the concentrated sequence of events in Rome and the extended barge scene, we are offered a breathtaking succession of thirteen scenes populated with secondary characters, with Antony all but disappearing until he resurfaces in Egypt. Time and space are fractured and the narrative logic is that of a chronicle.

ACT FOUR, Problem Play – The tempo is maintained with fifteen short agitated scenes; but what complicates the narrative here is the deliberately incongruous intermingling of martial matter with Cleopatra's histrionics, along with repeated, degrading disruptions of strategy by the see-sawings of love, and false or botched or actual suicides, infantile ploys (such as Cleopatra's feigned death) and the final inelegant confusion of the tomb scene.

ACT FIVE, Tragedy – Cleopatra, alone in defeat, suddenly has the play to herself and, rather like the Duchess of Malfi in Act Four of that play, is mortified into a nobler version of herself, purged of theatricality and rhetoric.

Shakespeare keeps changing the lens through which the story is refracted and in so doing achieves effects of profundity. His act structure is a mechanism with which to play out the story on a number of conflicting fronts, and thereby creates an unprecedented open-endedness of form. *Antony and Cleopatra* offers an audit of the possibilities of theatrical storytelling, and as a consequence can be diffuse in performance. Like *Hamlet*, it gambles on the audience's capacity to entertain the idea that no experience exists in isolation, and that the truth is best revealed through shuffling genres and switching focus.

The Naturalist Act

The risks of changing the lens are, of course, losing the audience in the process. Any play in a sense inducts and tunes the audience in to a particular emotional language in which they become more fluent as the action proceeds, and therefore the power of the play is cumulative. Yet the greater the number of acts, the larger the scope of the story, the more comprehensive its narrative language needs to be. Ibsen is instinctively a three-act dramatist, in that his plays relentlessly pursue a problem to the death. Chekhov, by contrast, is a default four-act dramatist in that his is a world of tonal complexity and layered subplots which will not admit a single moral focus. The fourth act tends to make closure more elusive – in Chekhov's plays, it offers a world beyond the climax of the play, as if at the end of *Hedda Gabler* we were to linger with the characters for another forty minutes to see how they survived Hedda's passing.

The pure aim of naturalism, epitomised by Zola's aspiration for a play to be '*une tranche de vie*', is the continuous, unbroken scene, devoid of authorial intervention, laid out like an experiment from which the audience draw their own conclusions. Strindberg's *Miss Julie* most clearly conforms to such a model. On paper, rather like Greek tragedy, it seems devoid of structure, with no scene or act breaks and the illusion of real time aspired to. Unlike Greek tragedy there is no Chorus apparent to segment proceedings; the play is usually performed without interval and runs at about ninety minutes.

Yet beneath the undivided surface of the play lurks the skeleton of an act structure. We begin with the wordless labours of the cook, Kristin, the intended of Miss Julie's paramour for the night, Jean. Kristin helps guide us into the dangerous game of seduction – she frames it, as an emissary of the daylight world of hierarchy and the absent Master; when she falls asleep the first act of the play begins; when she wakes we are emerging from the excitements of the second act. Also, in the dead centre of the play, Strindberg evokes the Chorus, daringly seeming to threaten an altogether vacant stage as mistress and servant go off to have sex, only to fill it with dancing, drunken revellers.

Another implicit vehicle of his act structure is the reiterated and transformed monologue, working like an aria to suspend time within the play: firstly as Jean and Julie trade veiled dreams of each other as a prelude to seduction; then, in the vengeful post-coital backlash, Jean reworks his earlier narrative of enchantment into something more sordid and Julie gives way to a vicious tirade of class hatred. It could be argued that *Miss Julie* is thus a two-act play, divided at its core by the act of coitus and the dance, with each half eerily mirroring the other. The first is the descent into love, the second the recoil from it; the first half, Julie as protagonist, the second, Jean. Even in its purest form, then, naturalism depends on the workings of an act structure; but it is here secreted in the text, the 'skull beneath the skin'.

Strindberg, in removing the signposts of the well-made play, simply set himself the tougher task of insinuating structure. His naturalist plays are notable for their seeming irregularity and intensity. In Ibsen's plays the war on previous conventions of act structuring is subtler; having inherited the well-made play, he stripped it of its tawdrier furnishings and adornments. Yet, as with Strindberg, there is an impressive singularity of purpose to the structures of Ibsen's plays after *The Pillars of the Community*, gradually paring things back to clear the ground for the closely observed agony of Nora, Mrs Alving, Hedda Gabler and Halvard Solness. One of the reasons that *The Wild Duck* feels so distinct from those plays is its more irregular act structure, apparent in the split in setting, moving from the louche, after-dinner world of the Gregers household, to the austere yet warm penury of the Ekdals. Then when we get there, that household is notable for its picaresque lodgers, and openness to digression.

Elsewhere in Ibsen the steady progress towards tragedy is not impeded by secondary characters or second thoughts. The real innovation in naturalist act structure is found in the plays of Anton Chekhov. The Chekhovian model of allowing a complex field of action to play out over four concentrated spans of time requires a rigorous form of internal organisation. Indeed, the naturalist act aspires to create a sense of sheer occurance which is very hard to pull off. In Ibsen's hands the contrivance is often all too visible as we move seamlessly through duologues enmeshing the central character in the tragic plot. Chekhov's achievement was to achieve that same ebb and flow of action whilst observing a notion of irregularity, thereby appearing to be more organic. The risk, as contemporary viewers of *The Seagull* noted, was the impression for audiences that nothing was happening at all, that time was hardly privileged beyond mere drift. Yet the internal choreography of incident that Chekhov achieves is in fact eerily acute.

Take *The Cherry Orchard*. Firstly, there's the clarity of the act structure itself: this is really a three-act play with an astonishingly superfluous epilogue. By the time Lopakhin gatecrashes the ball in Act Three with news of his success at the property auction, the play's action is arguably complete; yet the most memorable act is in fact the final one, with its dummy endings and almost comical lack of overt action. Chekhov nests within his master story (the fate of the estate and the impossible desires of Lopakhin for Madame Ranevskaya) at least eight other stories – they are worth listing:

A   Lopakhin's love for Madame Ranevskaya
B   The fate of the estate and the cherry orchard
C   Anya and Trofimov
D   Dunyasha, Yasha and Yepikhodov
E   Varya and Lopakhin
F   Simeonov-Pishchik and the neighbouring estate
G   Gaev and Ranevskaya's debates over the estate
H   Charlotta and the household
I   Firs and the household

Thus, taking each action in turn, Chekhov interweaves these tonally distinct storylines to create a constant variegation of feeling and action, e.g.:

ACT ONE
A/B – D – B/E/D – A/B/F/G/H/I – G/B – C

ACT TWO
H – D – B/A/I/G – C-D – B – C

ACT THREE
F – C/H/B – E/C/D – G –I –D – F – E/D – B/G/A – C

ACT FOUR
G – D/A – C/A – I – G/B/A/F/C/H/F – E – A to H – I

The acts, then, have a common structure: opening fragments and half-tones, building to a core ensemble cluster at the heart of the act, fraying again to a play-out of subplots. Act Three is the only exception to this, largely because it is the closest to the heart of the story and has a uniquely frenzied rhythm, evident in the whirling on and off of the dancers, the loose, boozy quality of the night. Notably, several of the acts end with a subplot which could be seen as the 'hope' motif in the play, the potential relationship between Anya and Trofimov, which structurally at least invokes the future. There's something very symphonic about this and indeed comparable to the compositional strategies of Chekhov's great contemporary, Mahler (compare this structure to the massive tonal complexity of Mahler's Ninth Symphony and there is a great deal of common ground). And to a greater or lesser degree it is shared with all of Chekhov's plays, which are structured around arrivals and departures and have at the centre of each act some abortive social moment: Konstantin's play in *The Seagull*; the whims of Serebryakov in *Uncle Vanya*; the various festivities in *Three Sisters*. In each case an underlying momentum of an act of expulsion: Serebryakov's dismembering of the household in *Vanya*; Natasha's in *Three Sisters*; Lopakhin's in *The Cherry Orchard*.

Naturalism created act structures that functioned as grand accommodating rooms for its stories; but, as in the households it represents, the apparently effortless action going on in them rests on the patient structuring work of the playwright, invisible as a scurrying servant. Ibsen, Strindberg and Chekhov, in their preference for two-, three- or four-act structures, reveal profoundly different approaches to that task.

The Post-Brechtian Act

With Brecht in the twentieth century (and also perhaps in the late plays of Strindberg before him), coherence of tone and form within a play is repudiated to compel the audience to engage in what Raymond Williams called 'complex seeing'. The act structure works like a tear in the very canvas of the play; its breaks are not disguised, they are emphatically visible. If Chekhov achieves this through interpolated contrast between stories within a larger narrative, Brecht aims for violent shifts in focus and register which preclude any singular way of understanding the story: the so-called 'broken-backed plot'. The clearest example of this is his *The Caucasian Chalk Circle*, which divides into at least three modes of storytelling: the Preface and Epilogue in contemporary Georgia; then the first half's epic tracing of Grusha's misfortunes; and the second half's abrupt shift in focus to reveal that story through the eyes of Azdak, the sardonic advocate. These ruptures in form might be modulated by the presence of a narrator, but generally they stand without commentary – the audience completes the puzzle.

Perhaps the most powerful post-Brechtian example of this dramaturgy is Caryl Churchill's *Top Girls*, a play so familiar and so exemplary in its politics that its form can be overlooked. Its structure is unusual within Churchill's own *oeuvre* as – more than any other dramatist – she favours the two-act structure (*Cloud Nine*, *Serious Money*, *Blue Heart*, *Light Shining in Buckinghamshire*). What the two-act structure offers is an embodiment of division: it can suggest cause and effect, before and after (think of the two acts of *Glengarry Glen Ross*); or, as in Churchill's plays, and indeed Howard Brenton's (*The Romans in Britain*, *Greenland*, *Magnificence*), two conflicting moments in violent collision. *Cloud Nine* exemplifies this with its split between imperial Africa and late-1970s Britain, presented in two self-contained acts, even plays, forced into violent counterpoint. *Blue Heart* takes this process further with two wholly separate plays (*Heart's Desire* and *Blue Kettle*) rammed together to create their own collective electricity through montage.

Top Girls notoriously prioritises theme over story, yet somehow manages not to dissipate the emotional ferocity of the underlying tale. Here again each act offers a different story-mode: Act One is an astonishing fusion of Shavian debate, dinner-party social drama and allegory – all played as naturalism, unfolding in real time. Act Two propels us into the world of social realism and the workplace play, with its sharp vignettes of life in the office, interrupted problematically in the middle of the act by a sustained naturalistic scene set in Joyce's garden. Act Three returns to the social-realist mode in full-blown form, an unapologetic kitchen-sink drama, as Marlene and Joyce lock horns in one of the most lacerating arguments in the history of theatre.

Given that this is accompanied by a backward chronology, with the last scene of the play being the earliest chronologically, you might expect *Top Girls* to be entirely incoherent as an experience. But such is the lucidity of the act structure that we are in no doubt where to focus and what to feel at any point. In effect, the acts function as a series of lenses, channelling our responses with supreme confidence, keeping Marlene in view as the organising principle:

ACT ONE – Functions as a long, often hilarious and moving induction scene; Marlene is viewed in the historical round, her achievements and implied losses and gains set against a parade of exceptional women from art, literature and history. This framing device makes impossible any glib criticism, or indeed celebration, of first-wave feminism.

ACT TWO – Anatomises Marlene in a workplace context and is infused with the hectic energy of neo-liberalism. All the different contemporary types of women swing in and out of view, defined by the limited demands of the employment agency. It's a tight world governed by interview protocol, as opposed to the free-flowing conversation of the previous act. There's a hint of satire and workplace soap to the logic of the scenes, which is where the power of Angie's interpolated scene comes in: with its long, meandering, monosyllabic logic, it's about as far from this world of chrome and leather as it's possible to get.

ACT THREE – Reveals that Marlene has her origins in that other world where we now find her, resolving the enigma of Act Two and at the same time validating the genre-shuffling form of the play as a whole. For Marlene lives in contradictory and conflicting genres (she's in *Nine to Five* and *Roots* and *Saint Joan* all at once), reflecting the violent transitions inherent in modern life as it whirls people from world to world. Yet the act structure's deep focus pulls Marlene back into a primary world of family, origin and class, away from the weightless comedy she initially inhabits.

Churchill's play adroitly draws upon the entire history of theatrical form to tell its story. Where it is in many respects complex, it is in others devastatingly simple. For instance, Act One is Saturday night in real time (pleasure/leisure), Act Two is largely Monday morning (work) interrupted by the ennui of Angie's Sunday afternoon, and Act Three is Sunday evening the year before. From 'Saturday Night Fever' to 'I Don't Like Mondays' to 'Gloomy Sunday', if you like – but perceptively using the implicit structure of feeling that underpins life in late capitalism. Similarly, the highly resonant, almost archetypal settings reinforce this simplicity of feeling – the rootless, eighties glamour of the restaurant; the sterile, impersonal yet equally prestigious office world, emblematic of service-sector-driven Thatcherism; the drab and yet substantial back garden and kitchen of an East Anglian council house. Each space has its own protocol and logic grounding the complex action.

Top Girls reveals the key role of an act in determining the shape and focus of a play, as well as the rich ways in which act structure can be deployed. We feel the presence of a strong act structure like a firm grip, guiding us forward and wrong-footing us all at once. In the movements of the acts, the deep structural presence of the playwright is sensed, working on us in a tacit, irresistible fashion, guiding us towards the writer's own vision of life.

Chapter Three
Writing Space

When I studied Geography at school in the late 1970s, it was a dull affair with lots of diagrams and bar charts. Yet increasingly, in contemporary life, geography is destiny; where you are is who you are. If you are born in Dhaka rather than Davos, if you're on the move from Pristina to Paris, if you're by a retreating glacier or an expanding shanty town, space matters as much as your class, faith or IQ.

This insight has long been apparent in plays, despite their inhabiting the 'empty space' anatomised by Peter Brook. The geography of a play often articulates its latent meaning; the geography of the scene, its dynamic potential. The former is about larger questions of place, topography, community; the latter about doorways, ownership, ways in and out. For whilst plays have a tendency to stay put rather than offering the skittish scene-changing of movies, their very inertia is often in striking contrast to their characters' desires. For Hamlet, 'Denmark's a prison'; for Madame Ranevskaya, staying on her estate with its cherry orchard is both unbearable and critical to her survival; for Davies, the tramp in Pinter's *The Caretaker*, Aston's attic is a refuge to be fought for at all costs. One of the key tasks of the dramatist is to locate their story in spaces charged with latent energy; and so often the failure of a scene or a play might derive from spatial inertia resisting the inner energy of the scene.

Hamlet again is an interesting place to start. Unlike so many of Shakespeare's plays, the evocation of Elsinore is notable for its lack of definition. In his well-known speech in Act Two, Scene Two, Hamlet appears to allude to the actual space of the

Globe Theatre where the play was first performed ('this most excellent canopy the air, look you, this brave o'erhanging firmament, this majestical roof fretted with golden fire'). Interior and exterior, public and private are fused – an effect reiterated later in Act Three, Scene Two as Hamlet and Polonius permit themselves an exchange of cloud studies within what appears to be an interior setting. Hamlet himself is fascinatingly 'out of joint' in relation to space as well as time. This Prince of Denmark, fresh from Wittenberg, is confined to a nation he yearns to leave, until he is expelled to England. Within the Court, too, he seems to have no place to call his own; his soliloquies emerge in the interstices of public scenes – so much so he frequently notes, 'Now I am alone' in advance. Every private space is prone to surveillance, either by Polonius or Rosencrantz and Guildenstern. Claudius's regime is all-pervading, which is one of the reasons the play has been so popular in totalitarian contexts. The most defined spaces tend to belong to women, yet these too are prone to invasion: Ophelia's chamber by her brother, father and then Hamlet, trousers down; Gertrude's closet, which (as has been noted) is not her bedroom but reception room, by Polonius and Hamlet. The castle, in its lack of specification, is as much a psychological as a physical reality, and so much of Hamlet's restless, compelling energy comes from his being deprived of his birthright – expressed vividly in the emotional outbursts that occur whenever he ventures outside (on the battlements, on the plains, in the cemetery).

As *Hamlet* reveals, space operates at a number of discrete levels within and around a play:

Performance context

The framing of the play in a specific performance context inflects and transforms its meaning. Aeschylus knew his plays were going to be bayed out into a daylit amphitheatre to 15,000 fellow citizens and scaled them accordingly, just as Shakespeare exploits the architecture of the Globe Theatre in *Hamlet*. Restoration comedies such as *The Country Wife* are utterly rooted in their original indoor, metropolitan setting, on which their jokes, allusions and asides rest. Increasingly, playwrights respond to non-theatrical settings, whether in the form of community plays for specific audiences or avant-garde projects emerging in abandoned factories or historically resonant sites. The original production in 1981 of Brian Friel's *Translations* in Derry Town Hall in the very heartland of 'The Troubles' is an example of how context can transform the meaning and add to the potency of a play. David Mamet's *Oleanna* was initially performed in a campus setting, which, as he commented, was rather like staging *The Diary of Anne Frank* in Auschwitz.

Staging space

Some plays implicitly suggest a particular mode of staging – traverse, promenade, end-on – which defines their relationship to the audience. A play's power to imply a specific staging format lies in its movement between spaces or its internal scenic workings. There is an interesting shift in Shakespeare's work from his early plays, written for an outdoor stage, to the hermetic, illusionistic quality of late plays like *The Tempest*, which seem predicated on masque-like, indoor theatricality; *Hamlet* is on the cusp of this transition, but its characteristic use of levels (the forestage for soliloquies, the under-stage for the Ghost and cemetery), depends upon the possibilities of the thrust stage. Roy Williams's *Days of Significance* was, in its first production, performed in promenade, and in its dramatising of the bedlam of binge-drinking squaddies in a market town, seems well suited to such a dispersed aesthetic.

Generic space

Stephen Jeffreys has noted that the primary decision about space, given theatre's inherent limitations, is whether to obey the logic of unified and unchanging space or to shift space frequently. He also points out that each shift in scene creates a diminution in intensity of focus. In theatre, the number of such changes determine whether the story feels cool and diffuse or hot and intense. So real-time, single-setting plays are often referred to as 'pressure-cooker plays', in contrast to the more fragmentary, diffuse power of multiple-scene plays. *Hamlet* unifies its many settings through an overarching ambience of repression and the idea of Hamlet's psychodrama. *Edmond* and

Woyzeck, with their sparely evoked worlds that are swiftly abandoned, constantly wrench us away from their stories and thereby preclude the deepening of a single emotional response; *Translations* and Conor McPherson's *The Weir* invite us into an intimately recorded world which we will be reluctant to leave.

Scenic space

The workings of space within a particular scene or moment is the focus of the following discussion. The implicit and explicit impact of the designated space on the unfolding of a scene is the micro-geography of the play, concerning the relationship between the door and the window, downstage and upstage, the relative virtues of a tavern or heath as the setting for a particular action.

A Brief History of Space

Given the emphasis of this chapter on 'scenic space', it's worth looking at the changing meaning of space – and indeed place – through the history of theatrical storytelling. Aristotle's insights about the unity of space do no more than express a primary truth about theatre's spatial inertia, suggesting that concentrating the action in a privileged space is the canniest decision a dramatist can make. *Oedipus Tyrannus* offers the most lucid interactions between onstage and offstage imaginable: the story-geography of the play might be diffuse – swinging between the poles of Phocis, Mount Cithaeron and Thebes – but the scenic micro-geography is incredibly simple, as the action moves between the external, public world of Oedipus's palace entrance and the internal, private world of its interior.

We've already seen this wasn't the only game in town in fifth-century Athens; even in Sophocles' own work, such as *Ajax*, there are spatial shifts which might diminish emotional heat but extend the narrative range of the play. A truly diffuse and multipolar idea of space, however, doesn't really appear until the emergence of the medieval liturgical theatre, evident in the dispersed spatial logic of performers in pageant wagons, staging Mystery plays in York or Coventry over the course of a day. This model is then transformed in Shakespeare's hands into the spatial fluidity of the chronicle play, a form that re-emerges with expressionist drama in the form of the so-called *Stationendrama*, echoing the tendency of liturgical dramas to shape their stories around a progress through stations of the cross, structured episodically. Strindberg's *To Damascus* and Kaiser's *From Morn to Midnight* take a central Everyman figure on a quest through the symbolic stations of their society, rather like Christian's allegorical journey in Bunyan's *Pilgrim's Progress* – from *Vanity Fair* through the Slough of Despond to the House Beautiful; or, for Kaiser, through the city, encountering its institutions – the bar, the courthouse, the prison cell.

This structure was refashioned by Brecht into what he called Epic Theatre, where the story moves through space and time and incorporates a sense of history, appearing less closed off and inexorable. *Mother Courage* manages to range through thirty years of history and across the canvas of central Europe without degenerating into incoherence, because it is grounded in the motions of Courage's cart and conceived for a stage with a revolving drum. It is a play entirely without interiors, epitomising the urge of political drama, as Howard Barker puts it, 'to get out of the room'. Spatial fluency and frequent transition favour the socially focused story that moves beyond individual narrative onto the plains of history or the planes of metaphysics.

With the development of theatrical form, the inherent scenographic language of a play becomes increasingly complex and specific. Whilst Shakespeare's predominantly exterior stage necessitated an imaginative engagement on the audience's part to 'piece out our imperfections', it also enabled a more panoramic canvas for the action, unencumbered by the lumber of naturalism. In his plays, as in Brecht's, the characters enact and embody their environment, and the space transforms inside our heads rather than on the stage. The opening of *Mother Courage*, rather like that of *Hamlet*, epitomises this approach. The two recruiting officers on the outskirts of a town during a lull in the Thirty Years' War eliminate any need for scenic devices – their irritable impatience and their evident cold and discomfort quickly evoke the physical conditions they inhabit. In Brecht's late plays there is a profound humanism at work, because the world is made and remade in the characters' words and bodies, again and again; perhaps reflecting Brecht's own exiled condition, we have scenes at crossroads, on borders, in the places in-between. Courage has to carry her own home on her back; there is no place for the solid, bourgeois homes of naturalism.

Naturalism also had its own spatial ideology, with environment shaping its stories just as much as character does. The samovars and heavy furniture that cluttered its stages were there to make the sociology of the play explicit, showing a world of money and goods but also confining the action within interiors and boundaries. This partially derived from the Darwinist pedigree of the ideas of naturalist writers such as Zola, Ibsen and Strindberg: just as the theory of natural selection proposed that the environment determined the survival and evolution of species, so space and milieu in naturalist plays often determined their characters' fates. This is especially true of Strindberg's *Miss Julie*, which has an increasingly eerie and fetishised relationship to physical objects, culminating in the shocking last scene where Jean hypnotises Julie into killing herself with his razor. When Charles Marowitz and Steven Berkoff adapted the play, they wittily reduced its action to these fetishes (riding boots, whips, choppers and birdcages), and thereby made explicit its sinister workings. It's as if the bell that rings to announce the return of the Master is the Master himself embodied in an object, and Jean and Julie are puppets of the set, which they (especially Julie) seek in vain to flee. Chekhov's adage that the gun on the wall in the first act must go off in the third, expresses this determinism. When, in *A Doll's House*, Nora dances her tarantella dressed like an Italian fisherwoman, she seems to be enacting her own neurotic reaction to being buried alive in this household of Christmas trees and antimacassars; the slamming door of her final exit is a symbol of feminist advance, but also an expression of her enormous relief at escaping the house with all its solidity. In Ibsen's later plays, that slamming door gets more radical: in the last act of *John Gabriel Borkman* we find ourselves out in the snowfield, finally free from the nightmarish incarceration of the house with its age-old feuds and silences.

In this respect, so-called absurdist drama is only a more abstract expression of the same deterministic idea, taken to its logical extension. The proliferation of chairs and corpses in Ionesco, or the mounds, urns and dustbins in Beckett, reveal a world in which people are all too often the 'slaves of duty', as Ionesco puts it. Pinter's plays, with their deceptive nods to naturalism, reveal this even more clearly. The attic in *The Caretaker*, stuffed with detritus and an incongruous Buddha, the seedy seaside lodging in *The Birthday Party*, and the bleak masculine household in *The Homecoming*, with its only female touch the solitary image of the dead Jessie: all seem deceptively real, yet within the course of the play mutate into places of great danger and mystery. Think of the opening of the second act of *The Caretaker*, where Mick menaces the sleeping Davies with a vacuum cleaner. In its use of space, absurdism reveals its roots in surrealism, where apparently solid worlds morph into treacherous ones, behaving with the threatening unpredictability of dreams.

Theatre in the twentieth century found its conception of space transformed by the challenge of the dynamic geography of cinema; the stage's increasing inertia is a response to the hyperactive motion picture. Sarah Kane's *Blasted*, for instance, opens with a wilfully static first act set in a 'hotel room so rich it could be anywhere'. The implacable focus on dying journalist Ian and his vulnerable, under-age lover Kate, as they play out their doomed relationship between the shower and the bed, is a riposte to the fidgety storytelling of the cinema. Sam Shepard's plays are especially interesting in this respect, given his double life as film actor/director and playwright; like *Blasted*, his plays *Fool for Love* and *True West* relentlessly stay put – respectively in a motel and a house on the edge of LA. The incestuous lovers in the former play seem like big beasts trapped in the cage of the set, lassooing the bed and hammering the walls. In *True West*, the two brothers steadily wreck the bland hygiene of their mother's home; the closing image of them frozen in the middle of a fight, one strangling the other with a telephone cable, contrasts with the dreams and ideals of the conventional Western they seek to peddle and trade in, with its promise of movement, eloquently demonstrating how theatre repudiates cinema's spatial freedoms.

Equally, the new geography of globalisation apparent in *Blasted* and suggested in *True West*, with its image of a world of suburbs with interchangeable streets and houses, reveals the prevalence in modern life of what French sociologist Marc Augé has called the geography of 'non-places'. Mark Ravenhill's *Shopping and Fucking* maps this disposable landscape dispassionately – the play is clearly set in London, yet, other than the nightclub, Annabelle's, this context is not specified, as the actions in the play take place in a sort of 'anytown'. Gary, the vulnerable rent boy who offers himself for the ultimate 'cut' of sadomasochistic sex, clearly has a regional lineage, and is the only character granted any trace of dialect or cultural context. Elsewhere, whilst the scenes jump across the city in a way that echoes Expressionism, this is truly a geography of nowhere: Mark's flat has no distinguishing features; Brian's agency, where Lulu auditions, feels like a front; Mark and Gary have their liaison in a perfunctory space over an arcade, only signalled by the tinkle of money in a slot machine. In this context, where towns become clone towns, and malls and gated communities from Rio to Rugby are identical, theatre, given the fact it takes place in a unique setting, becomes a quiet act of resistance, whatever is staged. All environments are now inter-penetrated by other worlds and it's impossible to re-forge the isolated, self-sufficient worlds that underpinned the plays of Ibsen or Synge. Indeed, in Martin McDonagh's Galway plays, including *The Beauty Queen of Leenane* and *The Cripple of Inishmaan*, the seemingly isolated community is shot through with brand names, references to sitcoms and the incursions of film-makers. Recent Irish and Scottish playwriting has excelled at creating a vivid sense of place and locality – from Billy Roche's Wexford to Conor McPherson's Dublin to Chris Hannan's Glasgow.

The inner concerns of a play are revealed by its geography and by its spatial shifts, because behind all such shifts lie journeys with moral implications; going somewhere else, or even just staying put, requires a choice to be made. Shakespeare's Lear moves from the Court to the heath, from interior to exterior, from civilised to barbarous space; Bond's protagonist in *Lear* moves from 'near the wall' in construction to another part of the wall which he attempts to destroy, and the argument of the play – that power and the need for security creates the threat the wall aims to exclude – is embodied in that journey. Lear's perfunctory execution as he tries to sabotage his own construction, just as he summarily executes his worker for sabotage in the opening scene, offers us an image of repetition as farce. In *Edmond*, the protagonist undertakes a negative quest from a sterile bourgeois interior to a kind of rapture in a prison cell. *The Cherry Orchard* moves to and from the 'room once known as the nursery', as if ushering us in and out of life itself. In *Blasted*, the arid security of that hotel room in Leeds is annihilated, as if the heath comes to Lear, with Ian sinking into a set shattered by an unexplained explosion.

Even a single-space play enacts such journeys, though on a microcosmic scale. The simple act of sitting down, of entering a room, of opening a window, can reverberate as profoundly as a sojourn on the heath. Think of Synge's harrowingly condensed *Riders to the Sea*, its domestic interior tended by women, its harbingers of doom glimpsed from the window, its laying out of the dead and its crowds of keening mourners at the close: the tiny croft draws into its meticulously itemised space a world of woe. Synge's time amongst the Aran islanders furnished him with astonishingly specific geographic insights such as 'the general knowledge of time on the island, depends, curiously, in the direction of the wind'. The crisp opening stage direction of *Riders to the Sea* conjures up, in a few deft sentences, a whole way of life:

> Cottage kitchen, with nets, oilskins, spinning wheel, some new
> boards standing by the wall, etc. CATHLEEN, *a girl of about
> twenty, finishes kneading cake, and puts it down in the pot-
> oven by the fire; then wipes her hands, and begins to spin at
> the wheel.* NORA, *a young girl, puts her head in at the door.*

We could be in a museum of ethnography (although that 'etc.' is telling); but Synge's opening image is active and taut with potential, rather than a dry diorama. This is a handmade world, a world held together by women, a world of work and things that function, a world of scarcity. The boards chillingly invoke the coffins necessary for the steadily depleted stock of men on the island. But what proves most powerful is the presence of the unseen wild spaces beyond the 'cottage kitchen', glimpsed through the window and embodied in the ever-increasing crush of villagers in the household as the rites of mourning commence.

Spatial Axes

Across all these variations of spatial aesthetic, certain axes tell us a great deal about the functioning of space within a play.

Public/Private

A play set entirely in private spaces will tend to express a disconnection from wider social meaning; one set entirely in public spaces will tend to inhibit the revelation of feeling and character. Thus David Edgar's plays tend to inhabit public spaces and rehearse public themes: *The Shape of the Table* in a conference chamber; *Pentecost* in a besieged church; *The Prisoner's Dilemma* in a series of high-pressure summits. This aligns them with the public nature of theatre but circumscribes the eruption of private feeling; at their best, therefore, his plays exploit the constraining of intense political passion by the public norms of the space and context in which the story plays out. In contrast, Noël Coward's plays tend to be set within the ambit of private lives, as even their titles suggest (*Private Lives*, *Hay Fever*, *Blithe Spirit*). On closer inspection this is less clear-cut, as Coward's spaces are sometimes hotel rooms or the permeable worlds of country houses. His characters may be released into the examination of their own feelings and concerns, but their protocols and brittleness suppress the full revelation of those emotions and transform them into comedy. It's no accident that his greatest work, *Still Life* (filmed as *Brief Encounter*) intensifies the problem of emotional expression by forcing its adulterous characters to leave the safety of their homes for marginal places such as the station café, the cinema, or a shared flat. As our social experience becomes increasingly zoned, with our lives played out in gated communities, private malls and on computers, the notion of shared public space becomes more problematic and the private more sealed off; yet the tension embodied in this axis is crucial to theatre, which in its very being rehearses the private in public. Enda Walsh's *Chatroom* teases out the confusion of public and private in the non-space of interaction on the internet; yet ultimately its cut-off characters encounter each other in the public space of a burger bar.

Onstage/Offstage

The aperture into and out of the scene of the action is the most critical source of pressure and power available to the dramatist; it functions like a tap that controls the play's energy. This is most apparent in the potential for exits and entrances, the sheer accessibility of the space from within and without; but also in the interface between what we can see and what we imagine. In *Macbeth*, the immense power of the first two scenes of Act Two derive precisely from this axis – the unseen bedroom in which Malcolm sleeps and the unseen exterior of the castle. The toing and froing of Macbeth to that chamber, followed by Lady Macbeth's completion of his deed, and the invoked sense of the sleeping castle around them, is charged with kinetic energy and the fear of discovery. Martin Crimp's *The Country* also exploits this axis to great effect, through the physical embodiment of the offstage world in the form of the phone, and through the disturbing way in which Corinne senses the presence of a woman in an unseen room, brought back to the house by her husband, Richard. His comings and goings to shower, intermittently answering and evading her relentless questions, the brash interruptions of the phone and the unseen darkness of the 'country' beyond the house, all place a thriller-like pressure in the events unfolding onstage. Indeed, much of the action of the play serves simply to explore the meaning of unseen events and places.

Open/Closed

Whether the space has an inherent function assigned to it by convention, or has a more open and indeterminate quality is another crucial axis. Closed spaces are those that have defined purposes and protocols: a public toilet or a squash court, for instance; you can have sex in both of them but that isn't their primary purpose. Indeed, it's a useful playwriting strategy to play against a space's conventional function, cutting across the audience's expectations and lending the scene an out-of-kilter frisson or a sense of urgency. Open spaces are more open-ended; a heath rather than a field, a beach rather than a marina. Yet this unbounded quality, this lack of inherent function, can make them dramatically potent. Edward Bond's *Saved* makes masterly use of these distinctions to suggest the cumulative effect of the repressive environment of the city. The shared rooms in Pam's house, easily interrupted and serving multiple purposes because of the family's poverty (no nurseries here), make fraught places for the sexual play of Len and Pam. The park, however, offers a sort of counterpoint to this stifling domesticity allowing them a brief, poignant tryst on the boating lake before they are interrupted by barked commands from offstage. But the park's limited freedoms, apparent lack of hierarchy and ineffectual governance make it all the more menacing and lethal later in the play. In the infamous Scene Six, it serves as the perfect setting for a drugged baby to be killed by a gang of bored men. The wildness of their pack-like behaviour contrasts horribly with the genteel, social-democratic blandness of the park, the embodiment of civic culture. Both open and closed in its identity, the park, set aside for leisure in a repressive culture, becomes a locus for indolent violence.

Translations: *Deep Space*

Brian Friel's plays exemplify how space in all its forms can shape the work of a dramatist. After all, he has a very specific geography governing all his work, namely the invented burgh of Ballybeg in Donegal. Like so many great dramatists – and Irish dramatists in particular – Friel's sense of place is intensely concrete and localised. Yet as with Seamus Heaney's poetry, the ostensibly bucolic spaces of Friel's work are charged with historical trauma, from the besieged vacated space of Derry Town Hall in *The Freedom of the City* to the etiolated, repressed household of *Dancing at Lughnasa*. Friel brilliantly complicates the axis of private and public, either through turning a private space into a public one, as in *Translations* where Hugh's household serves as a hedge school, or vice versa, as in *The Freedom of the City* where the inner council chamber of the Town Hall becomes a squat for three hapless citizens of the city.

Watching or reading Friel's plays in sequence has an cumulative pay-off, in that the regional specificity which fires his imagination yields an increasing density of imaginative reality for the audience, comparable to Hardy's Wessex or Tennessee Williams's versions of the American South. Friel's imaginative geography makes both offstage and onstage reality feel astonishingly concrete and familiar. This specificity enables a greater complexity of feeling about place and identity, apparent in his characters' geographical circumstances – simply put, do they crave exile or wish to remain in place; are they émigrés or immigrants, colonists or colonised, landowners or land-workers. *Translations* is driven by these nuances of character and space, enacted in their relationship to the stage space itself. Each character's fate and identity is defined by his or her place on a spectrum between home and the world:

[63]

MANUS – Rooted in Ballybeg (physically disabled); ultimately exiled to Inishowen.

MAIRE – Rooted in Ballybeg but dreams of emigrating to America.

HUGH, JIMMY JACK – Trapped in Ballybeg after abortive journey to Sligo; live in an imagined world drawn from Virgil and Homer.

SARAH, BRIDGET, DOALTY – Rooted in Ballybeg.

OWEN – Émigré from Ballybeg, habitué of Dublin.

YOLLAND – Émigré from Norfolk.

LANCEY – Coloniser from England.

Friel carefully delineates the degree of belonging or restlessness in each of his characters as a way of dramatising a community on the brink of its demise. Place is equally conjured through behaviour and tacit rules: the casual cranking up of the hedge school – subordinate as it is to the other rural activities of the village and indeed to the degree of Hugh's intoxication – is expressive of what the German sociologist Tönnies called 'Gemeinschaft' ('community'), rather than the modern 'Gesellschaft' ('society') represented by the National School. The permeability of home and world, public and private, embodies this, as the work of the class intermingles with chatter about the village. The staggered entrances of the pupils and the seeming ubiquity of Jimmy Jack suggests this, as does Hugh and Manus pottering in and out of the classroom and their domestic spaces. The easy access in the first act is foregone in the last as the Ordnance Survey sappers crack down and impose a curfew.

Such is the subtlety of Friel's writing that every virtue contains its opposite. The tight-knit quality of the community is also evidence of a defensive repression; the erudition of Hugh is also an expression of stifling insularity. The play's most potent scene occurs when all the inherent values of the hedge school are curiously inverted, as Yolland and Maire flee the communal *ceilidh* and exchange incomprehension and desire in the darkened barn. Add to this all the toponyms, mapping and the extensive imagined geography of the environs, and the sense of place is overwhelming – any resistance to this world is disarmed by the sheer detail of presentation. And this of course is what the play is about, given that what we observe through the arrival of the sappers is the appropriation of that known and intimate world, and its entry into history – governed by a far-off state and ultimately robbed of its cultural autonomy, with the encroaching school and of course the loss of the language itself.

Looking closely at Friel's stage directions clarifies how he optimises his use of space in the play to enact its inner meaning. The opening image echoes Synge's country cottage in its anthropological exactness:

> The hedge school is held in a disused barn or hay-shed or byre.
> Along the back wall are the remains of five or six stalls –
> wooden posts and chains – where cows were once milked and
> bedded. A double door left, large enough to allow a cart to enter.
> A window right. A wooden stairway without a banister leads to
> the upstairs living-quarters (off) of the schoolmaster and his

son. Around the room are broken and forgotten implements: a
cartwheel, some lobster pots, farming tools, a battle of hay, a
churn, etc. There are also the stools and bench-seats which the
pupils use and a table and chair for the master. At the door a
pail of water and a soiled towel. The room is comfortless and
dusty and functional – there is no trace of a woman's hand.

The artful mixture of concreteness and suggestion here is part
of the appeal of this image. The space is rich in its use of our
axes; firstly, as noted earlier, it stands at the midst of the polar-
ities of public and private, as well as bearing the marks of lost
functions and current usage, so it is both open and closed, and
in that respect quite unlike a contemporary schoolroom, where
we are unlikely to meet a 'soiled towel' or 'lobster pots'. The
implied confusion of function (and Hugh will later note that
'confusion is an honourable state') is mirrored in the uncertain
status of ownership; the master has his quarters upstairs but
this is a communally owned and used space, which is indicated
perhaps in the 'comfortless' aspect and also the ease with which
characters come and go. The image that follows, of Manus
attendant on mute Sarah, coaxing her into speech, set alongside the oblivious Jimmy Jack Cassie buried in Homer, reveals
an ease of coexistence and a lack of rigid boundaries. The
charms of this haphazard ramshackle place can be tracked
through its impact on the English Lieutenant Yolland, who
enters it stiff and gauche, but at the opening of Act Two is dis-
covered, in Friel's words, 'at home here now'. This is physically
apparent: 'He is sitting on the floor, his long legs stretched out
before him, his back resting against a creel, his eyes closed.'
Given that this is only days later, and acknowledging that his
at-homeness is backed up by colonial might, this image reveals
how Friel insinuates the workings of space through behaviour,
and indeed the very disposition of a man's limbs.

The real-time unfolding of the play accentuates this sense
of solidity, even if the action moves forward over a weekend.
Weather, another key tool in the spatial repertoire, consoli-
dates this sense of the pastoral, with summer passing into
sudden autumn. Tacit codes of behaviour reinforce this: Hugh
after all is the host, his shambolic yet charmingly proprietorial

manner represents both neglect and pre-modern hospitality; the abuse of hospitality in the murder of Yolland and the shocking abrogation of Hugh's rights for colonial protocols in Lancey's invasion during Act Three is all the more striking for the hazy informality that came before.

Translations is that rare thing in modern theatre: an idyll, an image of desire offering a kind of transcendence of nationalism through unalloyed parochialism. What marks it out as exemplary is the way it expresses story through space and place in the most concrete fashion imaginable.

Woyzeck: *Fractured Space*

For a very different spatial logic, it's instructive to turn to probably the most important play of the early nineteenth century, Georg Büchner's *Woyzeck*. The honed, crafted nature of Friel's play couldn't be a greater contrast to the raw, sketchy nature of Büchner's. Owing to the premature death of its author at the age of twenty-four, the play exists in most editorial versions as a composite of variant drafts, and even its scenic order is in doubt. Yet in its spatial logic lies a profound modernity, in radical contrast to Friel's play.

Woyzeck was famously inspired by an actual crime committed in a small German town by a man also called Woyzeck. Yet what Büchner assembles in his play is a mosaic of space and action, as we are shown the external forces that drive Woyzeck to the brutal killing of his common-law wife Marie. It's hard to speak definitively of scenic succession in a play whose final structure will be forever disputed; but what can't be doubted is the author's intention of expressing Franz Woyzeck's inner as well as outer experience through the fragmented representation of space. This is playwriting as psycho-geography, the world shown as experienced by a dispossessed barber. The form of action implied in the play's structure, the chronicle of a man who belongs nowhere and owns nothing, precludes the spatial coherence of Friel.

Büchner tells his tale through a restless interaction of spaces whose generic resonance and tacit behavioural codes bear in on the action:

Natural spaces

Natural, elemental spaces – 'Open fields, the town in the distance', 'In a field', 'In a wood by a pond' – frame and interrupt the action, often to brutal effect, contradicting their usual, romantic associations. At the end of what is now considered the first scene, the town becomes audible, cutting short Woyzeck's attempt to engage his companion Andres in conspiracy theories, as the drums call the men to muster; and the final dreadful killing and suicide also take place in this setting, to the sound of the 'buzz of beetles like cracked bells', as Gregory Motton's version has it. Woyzeck's manic episodes – hearing voices and seeing visions – occur in what should be placid, even therapeutic environments, and again Büchner casts space against type.

Domestic spaces

This is a story where the protagonist has no home in the eyes of the law. Woyzeck is a mere guest in Marie's house, which is for him viewed from doorways and windows, despite the fact that his child lives there. In Scene Two (again in Motton's version), Marie invites him in, to which he replies, 'I can't. Got to muster.' Indeed, Marie is imprisoned in the very room where she succumbs to the Drum Major ('It's getting dark, you could think you were blind'), unlit except by the street lamp; cramped, comfortless and constantly under threat.

Military spaces

Woyzeck's days are played out in arid, masculine spaces of institutionalised violence, governed by the conventional hierarchy of the Prussian State. There is little comradeship there beyond the perennially baffled Andres, shaken grumpily out of his sleep by his desperate comrade, or playing witness to Woyzeck's pitiful audit of his possessions. Whether shaving the Captain or being beaten up by the Drum Major, such spaces only confirm Woyzeck's essential homelessness.

Medicalised spaces

The medical experiment the Doctor conducts on Woyzeck is evidence of a similarly depersonalised world where people are reduced to objects. The tone of these scenes veers into the burlesque as the Doctor, like a premonition of a character by Ionesco or Dürrenmatt, babbles incomprehensible fragments of scientific lingo, and Woyzeck is bandied about like a glove puppet. Healing is turned on its head, the Hippocratic oath forgotten.

Carnivalesque spaces

Counterposed to all these environments of repression and sub-jugation are the nightmarish zones of popular pleasure, the fair and the inn, where liberty results in intoxication and animal-ism. Here Büchner emulates the 'montage of attractions' of popular culture, dubbed by Russian critic Mikhail Bakhtin a 'car-nivalesque', inverted world, populated by travelling journeymen (who incite a pogrom and bellow folk songs), or the Showman and his 'astronomical horse' which defecates on demand.

Woyzeck, as is often remarked, presages both Naturalism and Expressionism in its social specificity and emotional intensity; space determines behaviour, as is evident in the most alarming scene in the play, where the Doctor and the Captain meet Woyzeck in the open street. Their previous encounters with him occur in constrained spaces where the rules of oppression are defined, but the street unleashes from them a pincer move-ment of verbal torture. The very open-endedness of the space spurs them on to a heightened cruelty, and the action twists and turns with savage unpredictability.

Büchner's promiscuous use of space confounded early attempts to stage the play in a naturalistic or even expression-ist way – during Victor Barnowsky's 1913 production, the audience spent more time gazing at the curtain as the scene changed than watching the play. In a further offence against stagecraft, spaces are often revisited moments after we've left them, compounding the action's impetuous, jarring rhythm. Yet this arrythmia is a theatrical expression of Woyzeck's splin-tered condition, and the brevity of the scenes necessitates a spare visual logic where no place is rendered in any detail, where possessions are thin on the ground, and where perma-nence is nowhere apparent. Woyzeck's hurried entrances and exits further express the provisionality of his world. In each space he enters, other more rooted and defined figures lie in wait, like entertainers in a show booth – so much so that they are confined within and defined entirely by their roles, as their names (the Doctor, the Captain, the Drum Major) demonstrate. The opening stage direction of each scene instantly determines its mood and tone, suggesting that the spaces shape even the words the characters speak within them:

SCENE ONE, *open fields, the town in the distance*:

> WOYZECK. Yes, Andres, the place is cursed.

SCENE TWO, *in town*. MARIE *with her* CHILD *at the window*:

> MARIE (*rocking the child on her arm*). Bum, bum, bum. Hear that? They're coming.

SCENE THREE, *the fair. Lights, people. An* OLD MAN *sings while a* CHILD *dances to a hurdy-gurdy*:

> OLD MAN. On earth we can't abide,
>   We all must die
>   As everybody knows –
>
> [WOYZECK *and* MARIE *come in*.]
>
> WOYZECK. Hey-yup, poor old man. Poor child, little child, sorrows and joys.

The succession of scenes, their toing and froing, makes us giddy, expressing both a bipolar world and a condition suspended between nature and culture. But here, as in Friel, writing in space is less about design or the actual physical environment than implicit codes and possibilities. Think of the first scene between Andres and Woyzeck, an alarmingly free-form and non-progressive scene where the two men offer parallel monologues:

> WOYZECK. Ssh! Do you hear, Andres, do you hear? Something's moving.
>
> ANDRES. Eating up the tiny shoots,
>   Eating the grass
>   Down to the roots –
>
> WOYZECK. Something's behind me, beneath me.

Were it not for the sudden call to muster at the end of the scene, this image of quirky stasis could continue, Woyzeck free-associating images of patterns in mushroom rings and the workings of the Freemasons. Compare this with Scene Six, where Woyzeck is largely silent, engaged in barbering, enabling the Captain's own idle musings to predominate; when Woyzeck is invited to articulate his own thoughts, it's only for him to be held up for ridicule:

> WOYZECK. [...] The Lord said, 'suffer the little children to come unto me'.
>
> CAPTAIN. What did you say? What kind of strange answer is that? He makes me quite confused with his answers. I don't mean He, I mean you.

In a sense, Büchner shows more clearly than any dramatist before him how space can be a character itself, determining behaviour as surely as any human character, and how those without any claim on it hasten from one zone of oppression to another.

The power of the play comes especially from violations of the closed functions of the spaces: whenever Woyzeck speaks when he's not bidden, when he reveals a human function in a medical context, when he offers a private confession in the barracks, when he remains sober in the drunken mayhem of the tavern, he charges all these functional spaces with a dynamic tension simply by being out of place. He exceeds their specified function and thereby achieves a deeper character complexion than the mannequins around him, who 'fit in'.

Woyzeck, for all its unfinished qualities, offers a masterclass in spatial thinking: it dictates its staging format through its inherently promenade quality (it doesn't favour end-on productions); it defines a specific emotional energy through its scenic organisation; and the geographic intelligence that informs it is beautifully calibrated to enable each scene to flash out with the intensity of lightning. For all the plurality of spaces here, there's no diffuseness of effect, because the environments are so apposite and so effortlessly evoked.

Theatre, for all of its restricted means, or indeed perhaps because of them, restores our understanding of the almost sacred possibilities of place. Plays, at their best, humanise the physical world, revealing its potential energy, and, unlike cinema with its literal, documentary eye, present space back to us free of its habitual boundaries.

Chapter Four
Time Codes

That theatrical events take place in time is so self-evident it
can often be forgotten. A play on the page after all exists in
space, not time, and is therefore at odds with the very medium
it operates within. This temporality is hard to discern in novels
which can be read in one sitting or in many; only music and
cinema have time at their core to the same degree as plays.
Plays and musical compositions share the fact that the
duration of their performance is synchronised with the real
time of an audience's evening; however, within a musical
performance, time in itself rarely carries narrative meaning in
the way that it does for a play. Whilst time is deployed within
films to create meaning, movie narratives are generally cut and
spliced, and what is screened has already been filmed and is
located in the past tense. Only in theatre is time so irreducibly
centre stage and, given that fact, the playwright's inner
stopwatch is critical.

   Time can move horribly slowly in the theatre when things
go wrong. For all the battery of stage effects and gold-scan
lights, theatre, if it fails, traps its audience in that failure and
offers them little in the way of distraction. Stuck in our seats
out of fear of the embarrassment of leaving prematurely, we
suffer along with the actors. Philip Larkin wrote once of the
giddy lightness he felt abandoning a production of *The
Playboy of the Western World* at the interval – leaving at
midpoint feels an especially transgressive act, like playing
truant from school, as it breaks the contract of shared
theatrical time.

Yet this is not to say that dramatists must manically cram their plays with incident to distract the audience from Beckett's insight that 'all theatre is waiting'. The task of the playwright is to create something that unfolds in time, that creates a sense of time's movement, but the motor is set to the tempo of the story they are telling. Plays malfunction when this inner motor outpaces or overworks its given events; a story that is stretched too thin over two hours might appear absurd if played in twenty minutes. There is no absolute notion of fast or slow in the theatre; tempo is particular to the story being told.

It's useful to consider how tempo is manipulated in film to see how much easier the task is there: the rhythm of editing or loud underscoring or cameras in motion can conspire to create a sense of development where there is none. We can talk about a film's kinetic energy; and of course in theatre, scene can effortlessly give way to scene, acts fragment into pulsing moments, lights can move and music can play – but finally we are stuck with the inner tempo of the scene, which stubbornly resists all such haste and diversion. Time is immanent in the very body of the play; when the French film theorist André Bazin prioritised deep focus over montage in filmic story-telling, he was in some respects aiming for theatrical integrity rather than inorganic manipulation.

The dream of real time haunts all theatre. Forced Entertainment's *Showtime* revealed this wonderfully in its opening fifteen minutes, in which a performer stood forlorn in front of the audience, bare-chested except for a belt of dynamite, its timer set to the hour of the show, rehearsing theatrical clichés ('Every story should have a beginning, a middle and an ending'). By offering nothing at all in terms of narrative the audience was compelled to pay attention to time itself. As noted before, the literal notion of real time demanded by Zola was rooted in the idea of theatre as an act of bearing witness, and the stage as laboratory; but the earlier classical aspiration, to find a story commensurate with the capacity of an audience to believe, reveals the fundamental showmanship behind the search for real time. The desire for unity of time arises from a fear of breaking the spell of theatrical storytelling. It was precisely this intention that Brecht resisted, labelling it 'narcotic theatre'.

In a sense, the true meaning of real time is the desire to tell a story without apparent artifice or cheating, to present to the audience events that seem to function without the intervention of director or writer. The authority of a theatrical moment, its authenticity and power to move the viewer to belief, is grounded in the exquisite sense of time possessed by the writer. Hence the appeal of the unfudgeable action that drives the tempo: the meals in David Hare's *Skylight* or David Eldridge's *Under a Blue Sky* that have to be cooked; the kettle in *Top Girls* that has to boil; the marquee in David Storey's *The Contractor* that has to be erected. In each case these specified actions are durational, fixed and must be served by a sufficiency of dialogue and a profound grasp of the rhythm of an action, of feeling, of experience.

Forms of Time

A playwright must possess the capacity to gauge and not overtax the audience's collective powers of comprehension. It's often noted that audiences are more intelligent than the sum of their parts and that elements of a script that appear obscure on the page become blatant in production. All the same, a cardinal error in dramatic writing is the assumption that merely to assert something is to conjure it into being in the audience's consciousness. Arthur Miller once noted that to truly enable something (an offstage name, the significance of a place or a 'term of art') to register in that consciousness it must be mentioned three times; yet that tempo of comprehension has accelerated. Why else do we sometimes find the once-baffling Ibsen a little laborious with his leitmotifs, allusions and clunky exposition? Once the audience feels the storytelling has become pitched to the bottom of the class, with stolid repetition in place of fleet narration, it grows impatient.

Time, then, needs to be considered at all levels of playwriting:

Duration of story – The relation of action and event to both evening length and genre expectation.

Duration of scene – The timing of the action in its units.

Duration of moment – The rhythm of feeling and gesture.

Duration of activity – An organising physical task that sets a limit in time.

Our experience of time has given form to a vast store of methods of organising and parsing time into manageable units – and playwrights draw on them all. There are units of clock time and diurnal time: seconds, minutes, hours, days, nights, weeks, months, seasons, years. These apparently value-free divisions nevertheless carry their own meaning; think of seasonality, with its coded meanings that permeate theatre. Winter is almost always synonymous with death and frozen feeling – in *The Winter's Tale* we encounter Leontes's cold rage at his innocent wife, and her apparent petrification into a statue; while in *A Midsummer Night's Dream*, the sexual excitement of late spring and early summer, of 'Maying', infuses the action. There are many ways in which social forms shape time into comprehensible sections:

Calendrical time

As above, this codes the time of day, month, season around the agricultural and folkloric calendar: Nell Leyshon's Somerset play, *Comfort Me With Apples*, set within a rotting orchard, seems built entirely out of those autumnal images; *Miss Julie*, like *A Midsummer Night's Dream*, is infused with the promise of sex implicit in a solstice night; *The Cherry Orchard* is governed by the shifts from excitable spring (Act One), somnolent summer (Act Two/Three), and then autumn and incipient winter (Act Four).

Festive time

Socially sanctioned times of 'enchantment': Eid, Christmas, Pesach; weddings, reunions, funerals, bar mitzvahs; May Day, Remembrance Day. *Twelfth Night* encodes this in its title, and the inversions of love and hierarchy in the household take their cue from the time of ritual. *Blood Wedding* is built around the structure of the rites of marriage – the engagement, the assembling of the trousseau. Michael Frayn's *Donkeys' Years* hilariously structures itself around an Oxbridge college reunion – the arrival of the guests, the drunken mayhem after the meal, the departures in the morning.

Functional time
Imposed and preset units of time determined by an activity with a given duration: workday, term, semester, lesson, interview, consultation, conference, shift, prison sentence. Alan Bennett's *The History Boys* revels in the free intellectual play of the lesson and is structured around a term spent preparing for the Oxbridge entrance exam. Arnold Wesker's *The Kitchen* is limited by the duration of the cooking of a meal. Fraser Grace's *Breakfast with Mugabe*, as the title indicates, is structured around a limited series of audiences a psychiatrist is granted with President Mugabe. debbie tucker green's *random* presents the parallel days of a family – their work shifts, their lessons, their home life – thrown into relief by a devastating killing.

Ludic time
[75]
An activity in time that is rule-bound but freely entered into: weekend, match, game, tournament, event, performance, meal, party, the holiday, journey. David Storey's *The Changing Room* takes its form from an offstage rugby match. Mike Leigh's *Abigail's Party* tracks a disastrous gathering designed to advance its heroine Beverley's social climbing. Jez Butterworth's *Jerusalem* takes place outside traveller Johnny Byron's trailer home during the day of the annual fair in a Wiltshire town.

Biographical time
A unit of time arising from the nature of the human body itself, through time and sexual or familial relationships: pregnancy, birth, childhood, puberty, 'teenage', coming-of-age, affair, career, retirement, illness, infirmity, bereavement. Tony Kushner's *Angels in America* is driven by its hero Prior Walter's descent into AIDS. Harold Pinter's *Betrayal* is structured by the listless backwards chronology of an affair. Jonathan Harvey's *Beautiful Thing* blends the rites of passage of two young men, coming-of-age and coming out at the same time.

Historical time

A rupture in time that indicates irreversible change for a community or family: war, revolution, famine, invasion, occupation, election, advent of a new religion, resistance, scandal, terrorism. Patrick Marber's *After Miss Julie* sets the action of Strindberg's original play on the eve of Labour's landslide electoral victory in 1945, making more acute the class struggle implied in the original. Howard Brenton's *Paul* tracks the epiphany of Saint Paul and the troubled birth of Christianity. Georg Büchner's *Danton's Death* documents the shift in the French Revolution from progressive aspiration to terror.

Most plays nest within themselves multiple threads of time operating in counterpoint. *Hamlet* is a good example:

Calendrical time – The Ghost appearing between midnight and dawn.

Festive time – Claudius and Gertrude's wedding; Ophelia's funeral.

Functional time – Hamlet's confinement in Denmark, enforced by his uncle; Claudius's public meetings.

Ludic time – The performance of the Players; the duel.

Biographical time – Hamlet, Laertes and Gertrude's bereavement; Hamlet and Ophelia's coming-of-age.

Historical time – The threat of Fortinbras's invasion and Denmark's time 'out of joint'.

A play's temporal effects derive from these organising principles, which interact with each other to create scales of pressure and resultant energies. Thus in the first act of *Hamlet* the unravelling festive time of Claudius and Gertrude's overhasty marriage is complicated by the foreshortened biographical time of bereavement owed to Old Hamlet, and further overshadowed by historical time in Denmark's preparations for the war necessitated by Fortinbras's imminent invasion.

Brief Chronicles or Moments of Being

Through its history, playwriting has swung between two opposing modes of temporality: condensed, intimate time and diffuse, chronicle time – or what playwright Stephen Jeffreys dubs 'closed' and 'open' time. These conflicting currents are evident in Shakespeare's work as he combines the cyclical time schemes of medieval theatre, in works such as the first trilogy of *Henry VI*, and the inherited patterns of concentrated time derived from the classical past, as in *Othello*. It is rare for plays to be so diffuse in time scheme as to be described, as novels often can, as 'picaresque', in the manner of the open-ended digressive stories of Cervantes or Dickens. Brecht, who flirts more than any other with those modes of telling in plays such as *Schweyk in the Second World War*, *Mother Courage and Her Children* and *The Caucasian Chalk Circle*, nevertheless fashions their apparently scattered nature around tightly structured episodes; the latter play pushes that epic mode to the limit in its journeying, restless first half following Grusha's travails (and necessitating Brecht's favourite device of the revolving stage), but then reaches back for a much more concentrated dramaturgy in Act Two.

[77]

Plays which range widely in time and space, such as Shakespeare's Henry plays or *Antony and Cleopatra*, appear diffuse and fractured, but are in fact held together by their inner temporal organisation – in effect, they are a miscellany of mini-plays, unified by theme, but disciplined around events that prevent the feeling of arbitrary time. Act One of *Antony and Cleopatra*, for instance, exemplifies this trick of conjuring a huge canvas of events through three closely observed moments in time, structured around the emergent news of the death of Fulvia, and animated by the idea of departure and arrival. So whilst the act shuttles between Rome and Egypt, the organising principle of this death being reacted to at both poles prevents any sense of open-endedness. Similarly, a play of real momentum such as *Henry V* parses its huge journey in time around critical events, which bookends scenes of anticipation and reaction – the speech in advance of the siege of Harfleur, the night before Agincourt.

As playwriting has moved increasingly away from its epic, storytelling role, rescinding the dominance of plot, it has grown more concerned with the dynamics of what Virginia Woolf calls 'moments of being'; it has in fact relinquished the novelistic for the focus of the short story. Woolf's phrase is echoed in James Joyce's notion of the 'epiphany', a moment when the divine enters reality, or, in Joyce's secularised terms, meaning is granted to experience, as at the end of his long story 'The Dead' in *Dubliners* when the central character, Gabriel, contemplates the dead lover of his wife. The sort of rambling 'baggy monsters' Henry James discerned in the nineteenth-century novel had their equivalent in theatrical melodrama – after all, the more frenetic the plot, the less space for psychology, detail and the super-fine pleasures that James developed within the novel. Equally, the predominance of detail coupled with the increasingly uneventful nature of life in modern bourgeois society has pushed theatrical realism towards the microscopic. Think of the work of Martin Crimp, the inheritor of a tradition of playwriting first evident in Coward and brought to fruition by Pinter, where the action of a scene is often merely the attempt to articulate the principles that drive it. The opening of Crimp's play *The Treatment* is simply that: an attempt to describe and at the same time appropriate a past event, as two film executives try to bully a traumatised woman into accepting their version of her own experience:

> ANNE, JENNIFER *and* ANDREW. ANDREW *smokes.*
>
> JENNIFER. So he comes right over to you.
>
> ANNE. He comes right over to me.
>
> JENNIFER. He comes right over to you. I see.
>
> ANNE. And he sticks tape over my mouth.
>
> JENNIFER. OK. Why?
>
> ANNE. To silence me. He wants to silence me.
>
> JENNIFER. To silence you.
>
> ANNE. Yes.
>
> JENNIFER. Good. What kind of tape?

Despite the paucity of events, the scene plays fast according to the inner tempo of the characters, their thoughts and insights leaping forward even as they confound each other.

Scenes move at the speed of thought – the thought of the audience and the thought of the characters. Crimp's characters muse over increasingly reduced fragments of reality, but their inner clocks are set to urban time, where thought is often released from physical being, and psychology proceeds as fast as warfare. Thus his scenes have a lightning tempo, because change occurs almost without warning – characters switch sides, reputations founder, realities crumble, because they had little substance in the first place. The sudden reversals of circumstance that rupture the perceived situation in his play *The Country*, where lies revert back on themselves and facts explode the expositional framework, create a rhythm of shock and rapidity that belies the apparent eventlessness of the scene. Take this moment where Richard, interrogated by his wife Corinne about the circumstances in which he came across a lone woman on a country road, becomes obsessively focused on an apparently innocent word which may in fact reveal Corinne's awareness that the mysterious woman is American:

- So there wasn't a bag?
- A what?
- A bag. A purse. Didn't she have some kind of...
- A purse?
- Yes. A purse. A bag. Whatever. Don't look so / blank.
- Why do you say that: purse?
- Why do you say it?
- Yes. Why do you say it when it's not English?
- What is not English?
- Purse is not English.

The tempo is neurotic, full of nervous energy, intensified in director Katie Mitchell's production. Interestingly enough, when the pair collaborated to buff up *The Seagull*, that same screwball energy of high-speed gear shifts, entries and exits, bordering on the hysterical, abolished all preconceptions of Chekhovian languor.

Acceleration and Deceleration

Quickness is often a function of genre; compare Middleton's *The Revenger's Tragedy* to *Hamlet* – the former is a blood-bolstered example of the revenge-tragedy genre, wherein events have a cruel, precipitous logic even if they are gilded with luxuriant verse. *Hamlet*'s rhythms are much more uncertain and halting, calibrated to the proliferation of thought at the heart of the story. Whilst the cliché is of a tragedy of 'delay', the play in fact sets contrasting time pressures against each other; in Act One alone:

- The urgent opening is full of foreboding and anticipation and begins in haste. It settles and clots with Horatio's arrival.

- Claudius accelerates matters with his cursory and decisive dispatch of business, Hamlet functioning as an intermittently effective saboteur. His soliloquy takes us into interior time, the equivalent of slow motion in the theatre. The threat of Fortinbras's invasion functions as an accelerant to Claudius's haste.

- The departure of Laertes for Paris and the energy of Ophelia's anticipation of Hamlet again raises the tempo, only for it to be dissipated by Polonius's digressive coercion.

- The encounter between Hamlet and Horatio unleashes the question of the Ghost again, whose galvanising presence reinvigorates Hamlet's role in the play and leaves the act with a freshly conceived project.

This type of analysis could be applied throughout the play; every spur and quickening of time meets some contrapuntal obstacle (Polonius's intrigue, Claudius's deceit, Hamlet's reflection) that absorbs or displaces the reawakened energy. Then the polarity of active, urgent time and meditative, introspective time gets completely out of kilter: in the last two acts we see Laertes's dynamism exploited by wily Claudius, the time scheme of the play ruptured by Hamlet's exile and Act Five's movement from morbid wit and zen disengagement in the graveyard, to spasmodic, inelegant slaughter at its close.

Time is truly out of joint in *Hamlet*, not least because it is punctuated with soliloquies which exist in suspended time, animated by the quicksilver transitions of Hamlet's thought. Yet it is a rare production that is dull or weighs heavily, largely because of the epic scope of that thought and its own inner tensions. Shakespeare's temporal spurs – the Ghost, Fortinbras, Laertes – are constantly felt even if intermittently attended to, and that is why, unlike *The Revenger's Tragedy*, Shakespeare's play exists in a temporal space of its own making.

The Art of Repetition

Stanislavsky became preoccupied in his later work with what he called the 'tempo-rhythm' of a scene, by which he meant the almost musical structuring of the action; it's a fundamental concern for writers in advance of the actor's labours. A playwright's rhythmic sure-footedness is the key to their hold on the audience and their capacity to create dramatic energy – but the components of how that rhythm is generated are perhaps more mysterious. Below is a list of elements that is by no means exclusive:

Patterning
Every scene in every play is built around a pattern of actions and gestures that determines its tempo. The most self-evident is the exit and the entrance; increasing the rate of egress and ingress intensifies the action and sense of urgency. Other patterns relate to the specific business of the scene: the comings and goings of the Ghost in the first scene of *Hamlet*; sitting and standing in *Miss Julie*; dancing and cooling off in Act Three of *The Cherry Orchard*. Reiterated actions provide a kind of temporal punctuation to a scene, and indeed to the play.

Choreography
The choreographing of character groups creates its own energy; look at *Waiting for Godot*, where the dance is either a duet (Vladimir and Estragon) or a quartet (the incursions of Pozzo and Lucky). Beckett's *Come and Go* reveals this even more

starkly with the structure of 3-2-2-2-3. The different character clusters generate varying levels of energy and therefore tempo.

Echoing

The reiteration of motifs, whether verbal or visual, are another way of manipulating the tempo of a scene. The last act of *Uncle Vanya* deploys this to almost comic effect as a series of characters enter from seeing off the visitors and settle to work with the refrain, 'They've gone.' This might be as simple as an incantation – think of the close of Jim Cartwright's *Road*, where the four drinkers chorus 'Somehow somehow might escape'; or in the two acts of Pinter's *Old Times* where Deeley and Anna compete through singing.

Artful repetition creates an inner percussive score to the scene. The presence of offbeat effects and asymmetries is made implicit or explicit according to genre – in naturalism such effects are present but veiled; in farce or theatre of the absurd, they might form the core of the action. Consider Ionesco's *The Chairs*: the opening is an image of exhausted stasis that feels comically inert, as we share the purgatory of Old Man and Old Woman becalmed in an unending, eventless marriage. However, as the unseen guests 'arrive', Ionesco ratchets up the tempo to surreal proportions, his hitherto senescent protagonists youthfully whirling around the stage in response to an offstage doorbell. The gathering momentum of the invisible guests' entries exerts a metronomic pressure on the action. As in a farce, repetition here functions like a mechanism, its mechanistic quality making the action resemble a puppet show.

Powers of Hindsight

These techniques create only the surface impression of momentum; more critical is the underpinning event structure of the story itself. The proximity of a crisis is crucial to the significance of the moment. Hitchcock famously differentiated between suspense and surprise by contrasting a film in which, unannounced, a bomb explodes in a restaurant during a meal (surprise), to one in which we see an unseen hand place the device and set the timer before we watch the diners arrive, eat and chatter away, oblivious to their danger (suspense). This distinction holds good for plays, and can govern the temporal tenor of whole works, especially those that reflect on past events where the historical outcome – unknown to the characters – is glaringly self-evident to us; in effect we know that there is a bomb and that it will go off.

The effect of hindsight illuminating moments of calm and granting significance to everyday life is evident in a number of plays, especially historical plays where the outcome is a given and we see the world on the cusp of change. In Brian Friel's *Translations*, the irony of imminent famine and depopulation hangs like a cloud over the idyll of the hedge school; similarly in another great contemporary Irish play, Frank McGuinness's *Observe the Sons of Ulster Marching Towards the Somme*, the power of prolepsis, that is the foreshadowing of catastrophe, charges the last scene, as the brigade prepare to go over the top to be annihilated, with incredible poignancy. The same idea informs the action of Nick Whitby's *To the Green Fields and Beyond* and R.C. Sherriff's *Journey's End*. In Simon Stephens's *Pornography*, the shared public memory of the London bombings of 7th July 2005 gives a dreadful charge to the laconic monologue of an unnamed suicide bomber as he approaches London. With large historical events of this nature, the inexorable approach of fate enables the scene to feed off a relatively slight degree of plotting. The audience will the play to stay the motion of 'time's winged chariot'. Here, as elsewhere, Doctor Faustus's plea for time to stop – 'Stand still you ever-moving spheres of heaven / That time may cease and midnight never come' – is felt implicitly by the audience, and everything acquires luminous significance in the light of what's to come.

Another form of prolepsis arises from the manipulation of the time scheme so that the end, in a *film noir* fashion, is implicit in the beginning. Historical and memory plays deploy this convention most frequently to extract the optimum amount of irony from the excavation of the past – think of Peter Shaffer's *Amadeus*, Brian Friel's *Dancing at Lughnasa*, Arthur Miller's *A View from the Bridge*, Michael Frayn's

Copenhagen – the shuffle to the footlights of the choric agent of memory has become a rather tired convention, but the harvest of tragic feeling it yields still makes it irresistible as a device. In Friel's play, the presence of Michael seems to constantly suggest more than we witness as we eavesdrop on what seems to be an inconsequential day in the lives of his aunts in 1933; yet as Rosie and Aggie leave home, Michael's narration shockingly flashes forward to their fates as émigrées in London, living in squalour. Miller's lawyer Alfieri, with his tragic self-consciousness, projects a pall of foreknowledge over Eddie Carbone's story that means we search for portents whilst watching the events.

Looking Backwards

Reversed chronologies have, since Christopher Nolan's 2000 film *Memento*, become mainstream; yet Pinter's play *Betrayal* or the films of Alain Resnais precede it by decades. What's remarkable about Pinter's play is its sheer durability, despite the dated social mores at its heart. Temporal playfulness is evident in several of Pinter's works from the 1970s, and can perhaps be attributed to his sustained engagement with Proust during this period, owing to his adaptation of *À la recherche du temps perdu* for Joseph Losey. In *Old Times*, written before *Betrayal*, this playing with time is even more treacherous than in the later play, which after all proceeds fairly steadily once the first shock of backwards motion is apparent. *Old Times* is more troubling because it seems to question the very nature of the present moment on the stage and refuses to adjudicate between now and then.

Arthur Miller once remarked that 'now' is the most powerful word in the theatre. Pinter, though, was perhaps the first dramatist to reveal that it is a negotiable term – that indeed the whole substance of a play might be the battle to control the present. By stripping away all the appurtenances of walls and doors and specifying features in *Old Times*, he foregoes determining *when* we are as well as *where* we are. What he reveals in so doing is how action establishes its own present. When Deeley quizzes his wife Kate about her old friend Anna, we assume we are in the play's present, that Anna is part of the past, and that we are anticipating her arrival in the future. The present moment is manifest in a sustained act of anticipation and retrospection; yet there is a figure of a woman onstage, if turned away from us. When she turns and unleashes upon us a torrent of memory from what seems to be the distant past, we have to assume that time has moved on: it's later, she's arrived and established. Again, the energy and authority of her speech places us in time and charges us with the energy of a livelier past than present. Time is enacted in speech acts, as it were.

Pinter's boldest and most disconcerting trick comes at the close of the first act. We have accepted the conventions established above, and the evening seems to be settling into an uneasy yet coherent narrative – then, without preamble, Anna and Kate speak to each other as if they were back in that mythical London past, before Deeley, before marriage, before exile to the coast – even whilst Deeley, unacknowledged and emasculated, stands by:

> ANNA (*quietly*). Don't let's go out tonight, don't let's go anywhere tonight, let's stay in. I'll cook something, you can wash your hair, you can relax, we'll put on some records.
>
> KATE. Oh, I don't know. We could go out.
>
> ANNA. Why do you want to go out?
>
> KATE. We could walk across the park.

Deeley is snubbed and excluded. The setting is implicitly changed (before, we were apparently by the sea, but now a park is evoked). Anna, the guest, now seems set to cook. Pinter creates in this moment a worryingly unstable notion of time, which shifts on a character's whim; transitions from one moment in time to another are not signposted, and the play thereby offers an embodiment of our true, non-linear experience of time. As with Proust's alternations between voluntary and involuntary memory, where the past lingers in the present, ready to erupt and displace it at any time, Anna's dive into the past enacts what Proust's fellow modernist T.S. Eliot called the 'pastness of the present'.

If *Old Times* is about the recollection of time, *Betrayal* reveals 'time's revenges' in an altogether more schematic fashion by tracking its central relationship from conclusion to source. The play examines an affair between Jerry and Emma, and the disintegration of Emma's marriage to Robert, Jerry's best friend. Here, the question is how Pinter can sustain our interest in a story whose end is known, and what the dividend might be of going against the grain of the audience's pleasure. Yet the play grips and isn't merely elegiac, partly because it obeys the logic of a detective story: when Emma summons Jerry to the pub two years after the petering out of their relationship, she sets him off on an investigation of what was known and what was not. The play doesn't simply proceed doggedly backward in time – it moves forward and then back, with each section in time possessing its own miniature crisis.

The play's most crucial and powerful scenes, Five, Six and Seven, proceed chronologically through the summer of 1973, the point at which the core triad of relationships is under most pressure. A paradoxical crisis is offered at the midpoint of the play's events, as Robert reveals to Emma that he is aware of her affair, Emma conceals it from Jerry, and Jerry lunches with Robert, oblivious to what he and the audience are all too aware of. Aside from such effects of hindsight, elsewhere the reversals in time reveal the flotsam and jetsam of unseen characters subtly affected by the affair – the children; the writers Casey, Robert and Jerry spar over; Jerry's wife. Pinter's scenes also suggest an emotional journey for us through calendrical time (from spring to winter via summer); ludic, biographical and functional time (snatched moments in the flat bookended by the school day, or work commitments with all the frisson of 'love in the afternoon'); the tension of the meal in Scene Seven charged by what Robert knows about Jerry and what Jerry is helplessly unaware of; the danger of the initiating seduction in Emma's bedroom in Scene Nine, the final scene of the play. The fact we are aware that the affair is over doesn't dispel tension in the play, which derives instead from undercurrents made visible in retrospect.

The backwards structure proffers a kind of deep philosophy of the elusiveness of experience. Jerry's story (for he is the hapless protagonist) is one of missed meanings and opportunities; all belatedly revealed infidelities shock the innocent party into a re-evaluation of the shared past. *Betrayal* carries that process out formally at different points for each of the three characters, and the time scheme layers up ironies that would escape detection in a forward-motion story. It also engenders that most powerful of playwriting tools, dramatic irony – bearing down upon each scene so that the audience is always ahead of the characters, able to compare accounts of situations with the actuality of situations, to set words against deeds.

The play is in that sense a kind of retrospective, even reactionary, audit of the dissipations of the 1970s – surely it's no mistake that the primal scene of seduction takes place in 1968, the heyday of sexual and social liberation, and that the real objects of betrayal, namely Jerry's wife and the children of both couples, are never seen but often spoken of. Yet the other impact of the reversal is undoubtedly to produce a double movement of nostalgia and cynicism: all the moments of true feeling seem located in the past, but they are constantly being belied by the betrayals of bourgeois deceit.

Days of Hope: Utopian Time

More subtle time-travelling is apparent in David Hare's *Plenty*, which is in fact contemporaneous with *Betrayal*. For Pinter, historical time is vague and distant, where for Hare it is motivating and critical. In *Plenty*, the progress of post-war Britain towards reconstruction is presented as a decline from the heroism and hope of the Second World War; or at least this is how Hare's heroine Susan Traherne experiences it. Finding a form to express this psychologised experience of time, Hare mixes elements of *noirish* retrospect with epic jumps and temporal shifts. We begin at the end of the story with an image of female violence against men, as Susan and her friend Alice stand over the naked, vulnerable body of Susan's husband Brock, assessing his penis; we then swing back abruptly to locate the cause of this event. The second scene, with its

[87]

TIME CODES

utopian yet comic account of the Special Operations Executive in action in France during the war, becomes a kind of idyll against which all subsequent ones can be measured. If the first scene offers the end of the line, the 'doll's house moment', as it were, the second offers the vivacity of youth and hope.

Hare's craft in this play deploys different temporal strategies. Perhaps most tellingly he reveals, as does Pinter, how the sequencing of the play profoundly effects our reading of events within particular scenes: promises and intentions at points of intensity or excitement are shown to wither, and Susan's inability to adapt derives from her refusal to relinquish the truth-telling of war in the subsequent peace. Hare presents moments of un-being, documenting the progress of Susan into middle-class entrapment and ultimately mental illness, risking a narrative that becomes increasingly frustrating as the play advances – experiences made even more painful by the power of the play's opening. The pathos of its close also derives from the revelation of the past's ongoing relationship to the present. Susan's sordid tryst with fellow spy 'Lazar', first met in Scene Two in a hotel room, dissolves, in one of the most audacious scene changes in contemporary theatre, to a prospect of a Normandy hill, where her younger self proclaims heartbreakingly, 'There will be days and days and days like these.'

At the same time as encouraging us to read all events through this emotional prism grounded in biographical time (of lost youth and optimism), Hare plays on the painful hindsight of historical time. We know that the Festival of Britain, with its intimations of a progressive future, in fact inaugurated ten years of Tory stasis; we know that Darwin's fears about the decline of British power during the Suez Crisis come to pass, and most of all we know that Susan is simply twenty years too early to enjoy the freedoms of the late sixties – freedoms which she and Alice foreshadow.

Pastoral Time

'There is no clock in the forest,' says Jacques in *As You Like It* – and the dream of withdrawing from time altogether haunts theatre, as well as forming its greatest danger. Moments that seem to loom out of time in Shakespeare's plays are both potent and exasperating: the end of *The Merchant of Venice*, the graveyard scene in *Hamlet*, Malcolm and Macduff in *Macbeth*. Similarly, the second act of *The Cherry Orchard* seems to hang in the air, in danger of collapsing in on itself; and plays such as Brian Friel's *Aristocrats*, Nell Leyshon's *Comfort Me With Apples*, even the opening act of Sarah Kane's *Blasted*, or the entirety of Jez Butterworth's *Jerusalem*, seem to renounce the narrative imperative altogether, lingering with the characters, forcing us to relinquish our urge for movement and action. In *The Tempest* – which, along with *The Comedy of Errors*, is one of Shakespeare's few real-time plays (the action taking place in the 'time twixt six and now' as Prospero clarifies, suggesting it in fact takes place in four hours) – whilst Prospero is busy, his enemies in the Court find themselves in a time of drift and unwonted self-analysis, forced into proximity, with the rigidity of hierarchy suspended. Pastoral plays adopt ludic or calendrical time as a governing principle, all the better to confront their characters with their inner poverty or past crimes.

The title of Turgenev's *A Month in the Country* proclaims the manner in which this is achieved, as does that of *A Midsummer Night's Dream* – for in both cases the narrative unfolds within a rupture of quotidian time, through festive time, thereby utilising theatre's own inherent promise of suspended time. As in the latter play, the problems of daylight reality simply cannot be resolved in mundane time, and the province of the night, with all its transformations and stripping away of human pressures, is necessary. Athens's problems cannot be resolved in Athenian time. In David Greig's *Outlying Islands*, the manic, beaky rhythms of Cambridge naturalists Robert and John are confronted with the dreamy, insular energies of Kirk and his ward Ellen, all within the frame of the month of their expedition. Yet the threatening realities of history in the 1930s are not entirely suspended, as it becomes apparent that the remote bird-infested isle, which the two scientists imagine they are inventorising for science alone, is in fact earmarked for an experiment in germ warfare; and even the apparently Miranda-like ingénue Ellen is in fact addicted to the films of Laurel and Hardy.

The two scientists find themselves confounded by the natural rhythms of the isle, as with *The Tempest*'s unravelling of the fixed psychology of King Alonso out of his natural habitat. After the hapless killing of Kirk, the patriarch and traitor, John comments: 'time has begun to evaporate'; a quality mirrored in the real-time scenes that become more irregular and unfathomable as the play moves forward. Greig confronts his urban audiences with a different dynamic of time, just as Sam Shepard tends to dissolve his active characters in the moribund tempo of the frontier in *True West* or *Curse of the Starving Class*, or Pinter maroons us in the profoundly treacherous time of Max's house in *The Homecoming*. The quintessential contemporary pastoral play in this respect is Conor McPherson's *The Weir* – framed by the slow stolid pub in western Ireland within which the action takes place, realised at the opening of Ian Rickson's original production of the play by the landlord's slow entry from a distant door and a night of foul weather, and his patient and meticulous preparation of the bar for its tiny clientele. The audience's need for narrative development is quietly disarmed as the characters dribble in, order their drinks and begin their colloquy. But with the emergence of Julia, the woman from Dublin, that hermetic hymn in praise of the slow is taken to a deeper emotional level. Having been buttered up for a near-eventless evening, we then find ourselves entering into the active inner time of storytelling, with each character telling a story, and each story in turn taking us further from our immediate context and into the inner reality of the characters. It is no exaggeration to say that the effect is magical, because, as in all great pastoral plays, here our outside concerns are suspended for an act of inner healing to be achieved. *The Weir*, and indeed all of McPherson's work, serves as a reminder of theatre's shamanistic powers of transformation, touched on so profoundly in Brian Friel's *Faith Healer* – it reminds us that theatre, like food, drink and love, should not be hurried, and indeed is an antidote in its inherent slowness to the restless superficiality of life beyond its doors.

Likewise in Jez Butterworth's *Jerusalem*, the finest play staged during the writing of this book, time and urbanism is once again suspended in order to evoke a primordial England, embodied in the nomadic, promiscuous, intoxicated life of Romany Johnny Byron, and now under threat from officious bureaucracy in the form of Kennet and Avon Council, who wish to expel him from his unauthorised roost within twenty-four hours. The play opens with a Bacchanalian moonlit rave, but then Byron's slow emergence from the stupor of the night, counterposed by the offstage muted revelry of the local town fair, yields a wonderfully halting tempo of action, animated by the arrival of Byron's young friends and fellow bacchants and, as in *The Weir*, the sheer mesmeric power of stories. Butterworth grants Byron such inordinate powers of language that the very flow of narrative seems altogether suspended; we are pulled into a more atavistic England of giants and old girl-friends and abrogated freedoms. *Jerusalem* is living proof that, in theatre, character can almost entirely eclipse narrative urges – three hours with Johnny 'Rooster' Byron disarm in us the need for 'action' and provoked (in me at least) an almost unquenchable nostalgia for an England that probably never existed.

Act Two

Vital Signs

Chapter Five
Dramatis Personae: Constructing Character

The Character Repertoire

Shakespeare is often deemed the quintessential playwright because, as Vladimir Nabokov noted, he created an astonishing repertoire of characters, understood in range and breadth, loved equally and treated equitably. Michael Frayn has observed likewise that in the best plays all the characters are right, that they all possess their own logic and are not ciphers or monsters. Whilst we seek the voice and presence of a playwright behind their many stratagems, in any play there is at the same time a promise inherent of a realm beyond individual judgement, an ideal democracy where all its clamorous voices get their say. I find so much of John Osborne's work intolerable because it flouts this promise, with many of his characters serving as mere foils to his hyper-vivid protagonists, whipping boys for Jimmy Porters.

But life is rather narrow. Most of us, playwrights included, carry within us a circumscribed dramatis personae. How many people do we meet in a single lifetime who we really get to know – perhaps a hundred? And of those, how many could we honestly say we understand? Of course, there are tireless networkers out there who collect people as they might dolls, reducing them to a surface detail or trait under which to file them away – X is neurotic, Y holidays in Brazil, Z's a former Marxist. As we grow older our social arteries harden and our address book is decreed full. We judge newcomers by precedent;

any veteran teacher will reveal how quickly their fresh new class is assimilated into old categories – the cheeky one, the wimpy one, the sycophantic needy one – in lieu of the complex individuality of little Samuel, Becky or Jack.

A play may be set anywhere – from the Dark Ages to contemporary London – but a writer's archetypes will surface just the same, drawn from the palette of their limited experience. A play that does not in some way reveal its author is a chimera. Often, dramatists draw on the same quarrelling extended family they inherit from experience. Think of Ibsen's archetypes:

Freedom seeker – Nora in *A Doll's House*, Hilde Wangel in *The Master Builder*, Osvald in *Ghosts*, Hedda in *Hedda Gabler*, Rebecca West in *Rosmersholm*, Gregers in *The Wild Duck*, Stockmann in *An Enemy of the People*.

Corrupt authority figure – Rank in *A Doll's House*, Brack in *Hedda Gabler*, Manders in *Ghosts*, Borkman in *John Gabriel Borkman*.

Emasculated husband – Torvald in *A Doll's House*, Solness in *The Master Builder*, Tesman in *Hedda Gabler*.

Ruined supplicant – Mrs Linde in *A Doll's House*, Mrs Elvsted and Lovborg in *Hedda Gabler*.

Gullible child – The eponymous Little Eyolf, Hedvig in *The Wild Duck*.

These figures are all partial versions of the writer, who was himself catapulted from an origin in debt and penury to affluent exile but personal stasis. In medieval 'psychomachian' dramas, such as *The Castle of Perseverance*, characters personify virtues or vices, allegorically battling for supremacy within one mind or soul. Rather less crude allegories underpin all plays, which externalise the dramatist's own inner turbulence in the hope that they will resonate with those of a wider public. In the work of some playwrights this is all too evident: Tennessee Williams or Arnold Wesker palpably form their plays from the unfinished battles of their public and private lives, resorting to a constant character repertoire. Critics and biographers like to follow the maze from character to real-life counterpart, reducing each play to the equivalent of a *roman-à-clef*. But even a writer like Mike Leigh, who combs the memories and experiences of his acting collaborators for new stories and people, creates characters in all his plays who bear rather more than a passing resemblance to each other (the ambitious lower-middle-class woman, the rooted working-class man, the manic yuppie, the inarticulate loner, the pedantic bore). A dramatist's experiences speak loudly through the voices and selves they conjure up from within their imagination, which in itself is a menagerie of all those influences that have pressed down upon them.

Reading Character

In *Aspects of the Novel*, E.M. Forster divided characters up into 'rounded' and 'flat'; the former gifted with inner life and the possibility of transformation, the latter invariably seen only from outside and limited to a comic existence. 'Flat' is to some extent the default mode for the theatre, which is, finally, a behavioural form. Plays offer a model for what philosophers call the 'problem of other people's minds' in action; we infer a character's inner life from the sum of their external actions. Ever since Henry James, the novel has increasingly borrowed the theatrical conception of character as something fragmentary, glimpsed rather than fully known. As Strindberg wrote – in one of the most profound discussions of theatrical character ever penned, his introduction to *Miss Julie* – 'character' is not essence but existence. His 'wild oscillating beings' demonstrate that characters are made not born, and whilst the external world may form part of their determining, for the audience they are no more nor less than the sum of their actions.

The opening of a play is rather like the experience of going to a party where you don't know anyone. A parade of people stands before you. A woman approaches who seems congenial; she offers you a drink, she's clearly interested in you; she disappears off to the kitchen and, while you wait, the slightly surly-looking fat man on the sofa observes, 'Jenny'll drop you in half an hour.' Naturally, you recoil from him, but you note an older woman by the window smiling at his bitchiness: 'Forgive Jim, he's her ex.' Okay, you now start to take pity on Jim, who's clearly had a few, and when Jenny returns with your bottle and notes rather crisply that 'We only drink fair-trade wine here,' you sidle over to Jim, only to see him get up off the sofa and retreat with Jenny for a smoke. Within minutes your loyalties have shifted entirely and your initial judgements been unpicked. The evidence you've drawn on ranges from physical appraisal, personal interaction and interpersonal commentary. So it is with a play.

Every member of the audience is rather like Elizabeth Bennet in *Pride and Prejudice*, disliking Darcy and falling for Wickham – the play of appearance and reality is incessant and endlessly engaging. Character unfolds in time, and first impressions will be qualified by later ones; plays may begin with stereotypes but they cannot remain content with them.

There are ways a playwright can make this confusing and often baffling point of entry into a play less arduous for the audience: think of Shakespeare's openings, where servants or secondary figures function as gossiping curtain-raisers to the characters we are about to meet. But the real craft is to configure events to both complicate and illuminate the characters. Consider how Edward Bond's *Lear* reconfigures Shakespeare's *King Lear*. Shakespeare begins his play with some opaque dialogue between Kent and Gloucester, cut short by Lear's precipitate and dynamic entrance; he lets us fall for the emollient words of Goneril and Regan, and we share their father's puzzlement at Cordelia's terseness. In contrast, Bond offers us a kaleidoscope of appraisals of his King. Firstly, we witness an industrial accident, which colours our feelings about Lear's key defence project, the wall. The inhuman response of the military figures overseeing the workers suggests we're not about to meet a liberal philanthropist, but neither are we in a serenely functioning authoritarian state. Everything feels hasty, dangerous and out of control. Then the royal party enter. Bond could have made his work easier by staggering their entrances, but instead everyone crowds on (Lear, Lord Warrington, an Old Councillor, an Officer, an Engineer, and Lear's daughters Bodice and Fontanelle). Their fractured commentaries suggest a nervousness and instability, confirmed by Lear's own capricious behaviour:

BODICE (*to* FONTANELLE). We needn't go on. We can see the
    end.

ENGINEER. The chalk ends here. We'll move faster now.

COUNCILLOR (*looking at his map*). Isn't it a swamp on this
    map?

FONTANELLE (*to* BODICE). My feet are wet.

LEAR (*points to tarpaulin*). What's that?

ENGINEER. Materials for the –

WARRINGTON (*to* FOREMAN) Who is it?

FOREMAN. Workman.

WARRINGTON. What?

FOREMAN. Accident, sir.

The pattern of non sequiturs, the hastiness of the lines, the
peremptory switches in focus again inform our judgements of
Lear. The subsequent botched and delayed execution of a soldier, summarily accused of sabotage, compounds further our
sense of being in a world characterised by incompetence and
petulance. Bond's whole philosophy of character is apparent in
the manner in which he places his figures in their social context, revealing them as a group – through actions rather than
dwelling on their distinctiveness.

    This terrifying scene is a masterclass in swift character evo-
cation and illuminates the fact that, in theatre, character is not
only action but also reaction. The most pertinent mode in
which we can evaluate character is through power and protocol. The sycophants around Lear suggest a compliant, turgid
Court which stands in contrast to his wayward, childlike rhetoric. Uneasy buck-passing and, in the case of his daughters,
snide resistance, imply a realm of loveless obedience and formality on the brink of insolence.

Complexity in Character

Peter Brook's reworking of *Hamlet*, *Qui est là*, memorably
reduced it to a series of variations on the first line of the play –
'Who's there?' – and suggested that this question drives all theatre. So much of the work of playwriting is unfolding
characters, complicating and thereby 'deepening' stereotypes.

The presentation of character in theatre is about individuating voices and actions that separate one figure from another, and creating the illusion of inwardness. Yet character only emerges through interaction; like 'shifters' in language (a term coined by linguist Otto Jespersen for words such as 'I' or 'there', which possess no meaning beyond the context in which they appear), dramatic character is defined by situations. Determining the 'meaning' of a character is as futile as trying to have the final word on any individual; they're simply the sum of a set of inter-actions within the play. The very fact that characters bear an identity separable from the scenarios that contain them is often what the play is in fact about – they are bigger than the facts of the story. Great characters have too much 'character' for their story, in effect refusing to remain functional like minor ones. If Macbeth remained the loyal soldier rather than aspiring to the throne, there'd be no *Macbeth*; he is a minor character intent on becoming a major one. In life, characters of such complexity can be insufferable; in plays they're irresistible.

Central characters are problem figures with exemplary fates, uncontainable within fixed social structures and sanc-tioned roles. *Hamlet* clarifies this. Here the protagonist refuses to be defined by any of the roles assigned to him. Those roles ('sweet prince', loyal son, student, lover, nephew) have been rendered intolerable by the actions of Claudius and Gertrude – is Hamlet now his father's or his mother's son? Is he heir to the throne or a puppet prince? Is he Ophelia's lover or her preda-tor? The play becomes even more interesting through Hamlet's inability to inhabit the role of the revenger, a role conferred on him by genre expectations. The number of roles that he's inca-pable of playing explain Hamlet's endless playability – it's simply impossible to have the last word on him.

Hamlet's complexity works on all levels, the function of even secondary characters in the play is rarely clear. Are Rosencrantz and Guildenstern reconciled to their function as spies? Is Ophelia in love with Hamlet or is she merely her father's stooge? How culpable is Gertrude? How are we to take Claudius's apparent remorse? And is the Ghost of Old Hamlet a devil or the genuine article? Elsinore seems blighted by duality. As critic Stephen Greenblatt notes, an 'opacity' of motive and situation lies at the heart of the play, making problematic its status as revenge drama with all its stereotypical gestures. Hamlet's tendency to blot out the play around him, generating clichés such as 'the procrastinating prince', nevertheless reveals how narrative and stereotype march in step: a simpler hero would yield a simpler, plot-driven play. By interrogating the nature of 'roles', the play inaugurates a sort of anti-theatre, dissolving certainties and returning again and again to questions.

Plays undermine fixed notions of identity. They have always been existentialist in the sense that they present character in action and offer existence before essence. In Athenian tragedy, the foundation myths of democracy were subjected to relentless scrutiny by Aeschylus, Sophocles and Euripides, challenging their audiences with what French classicist Jean-Pierre Vernant called 'myth through the prism of the citizen'. Myth is not psychological; it depends on stereotype or archetype, on physically conceived characters, and a world of action inhabited by heroes and monsters. Tragedy puts the hero in a sceptical, more domestic context; brings them home, as it were, trapping them in a web of social complexity, like Agamemnon in Clytemnestra's net. Euripides, for instance, examines Heracles, Jason, Odysseus and Hecuba in truly unflattering close-up. In *Hecuba* he asks 'Who is Hecuba?' Is she a benighted, exiled Trojan Queen, worthy of our compassion, a victim of the politicking of Odysseus? Or is she the so-called bitch of Canossa, who ruthlessly murders children? In *Hecuba* she's both – her sufferings aren't simply causes for her latter actions, or at least they are incommensurate with them; she's transformed before our eyes into her opposite. By presenting Hecuba's transformation in continuous time – seen through her interactions with her daughter Polyxena, resisting the wiles of Odysseus, importuning Agamemnon for revenge and then slaughtering Polymestor's sons – Euripides offers an insight that comes to govern later theatre: that character is, to use anthropologist Mary Douglas's terms, 'positional' not 'personal'; that we are determined as well as determining.

Euripides' play presents a set of hypothetical conditions enabling us to examine what happens to those from whom 'all is taken'.

Tragedy works like a trial or tribunal: if we detect what Keats would call 'a palpable intent', we dismiss it as skewed or rigged. The characters demand fair treatment and pure judgement even if that is illusory; they have no truck with stereotypes; they will have their 'day in court'. And their hope arises from the fact that plays are inherently dialogic: for every position stated, a counterposition is posited; for every thesis concerning a character, a contrary one is supplied. Clytemnestra engineers the murder of Agamemnon – but then again she did suffer the loss of Iphigenia. The Russian critic Mikhail Bakhtin's term 'dialogicity', coined in his study of Dostoevsky's novels, is even more pertinent to plays, with their reversals, mirroring incidents and scenarios of suspended judgement.

Comic Character

[102]

A brief survey of comedy offers a movement in the other direction. Comic characters in plays from *Lysistrata* to *What the Butler Saw* remain confined to role in order for the plot to predominate. This is evident in the largely ensemble focus of so many comedies – even in those of Shakespeare, who pushes the possibilities of the form to the limit. An early comedy such as *The Comedy of Errors*, derived from a Plautine farce, might flirt with non-comedic elements – such as the threatened death of the father Egeon in the rather earnest opening, or indeed the darker sentiments of Adriana and Luciana about love and men – but effectively character serves plot. Despite the fact that the drubbings and beatings doled out to both Dromios place them closer to our sympathies, there's never a question of them exceeding their function as the benighted servant; for Dromio of Syracuse, his experiences of Ephesus don't disturb the essential interplay between him and his master Antipholus. No one, in fact, aspires to dominate the middle ground of the play; the plot is not driven by aspiration, but by circumstance. Comedy, especially, inhabits a world in which things happen to people, rather than one in which they shape their own destinies.

A Midsummer Night's Dream is likewise constructed around essentially static worlds of character, with only Titania and Oberon within the fairy realm and Nick Bottom threatening to move beyond their orbit. The four lovers, whilst their predicament strips back their civilities to reveal sharper, edgier potential, are ultimately at mercy of the workings of magic and the plot. Bottom might be 'translated', but it is only temporarily. The final, socially obnoxious but hilarious act of hymeneal performance in Act Four revels in the separateness of worlds that look dangerously interfused in the previous act. As in Dickens, comedy confines character to predictable tics and gestures; Bottom's spoonerisms, Puck's puckishness and Theseus's serene authority quickly mark them out and equip them to move the plot on. The wonderful, troubling muddle in the midst of the play – as Lysander abandons Hermia, Helena becomes desired by all who see her, Titania falls for Bottom – is funny precisely because it takes static characters briefly out of their confines and compels them to change; the task of the play is then to reverse that utterly.

Irreversible change is not on the agenda for comedy, and therefore complexity in character is not available. Within Shakespeare's own writing, comedy in its purer forms becomes increasingly untenable, as he applies to it his profound grasp of character. With the pain and travails of figures such as Malvolio in *Twelfth Night*, we move beyond the closed circuit of comedy derived from farce or *Commedia* into the dangerous realm of psychological nuance. The late romances are the answer: in plays such as *The Tempest* and *The Winter's Tale*, remnants of comedy linger on in the darker projects and the complexity of figures such as Prospero and Leontes. Caliban's aspiration to complexity and his attempt to usurp Prospero might be grotesque, but it is hardly funny; it's as if Bottom had really fallen for Titania and imagined himself thereafter fit to sleep with whomever he chose.

The Uses of Stereotype

Modern drama, sceptical about representation in itself, and intent on revealing the presence of society in the individual through representative characters as well as unique nuanced psychologies, placed new pressures on characterisation, and offered a new role for stereotype. Its re-emergence in the work of Brecht and others was an admission that drama had become increasingly ill-suited to representing the huge social forces underlying any particular story. The German critic Peter Szondi theorises the process brilliantly in *Theory of the Modern Drama*: the modern play became unable to tell the whole story within a single plot because modern realities were no longer self-sufficient. As T.S. Eliot said of poetry, to capture the complexity of experience, 'difficulty' was necessary. Somehow history, the economy, the new psychology, needed to become visible in the action, which could no longer be presented as unmediated.

Again, Büchner's *Woyzeck* was prescient in this matter. A question raised but dodged in the trial of the real-life Woyzeck was the degree of responsibility that could be attributed to him – was he culpable for stabbing Widow Woost, or might a plea of diminished responsibility be accepted in his case? Clarus, the testifying medical scientist, thought him culpable, but Büchner, a natural scientist by training, author of a tract on the cranial nerves and a proto-Marxist, thought otherwise. The resulting play bears within it the difficulty of representing both the internal and external meanings of experience at one and the same time – the confidence with which earlier drama offered us surfaces from which we derived depths was no longer possible. So, forty years before Naturalism and sixty years ahead of Expressionism, Büchner anticipates both movements in his representation of character. His solution to the challenge of combining social critique with psychological anatomy is to provide two tiers of characterisation which invert the history of theatre hitherto, in that the bourgeois characters are confined to stereotype, whereas the working-class characters are complex and ambivalent. The Doctor and the Captain are socially representative, vehicles of hierarchy imposed through rigidly policed stereotypes. For the Captain, Woyzeck represents an anarchic, amoral abjection ('you're a decent man – but you've got no morals,' he opines in a wonderful oxymoron). The Captain's package of social assumptions, which he projects onto Woyzeck, reveals the retreat of the social imagination as the hierarchies of bourgeois society harden in the early nineteenth century. Certainly, the Doctor, with his experiments on Woyzeck (chillingly foreshadowing the world of concentration camps), is another example of the bourgeois attempt to fix those beneath into object categories. The irony is that both characters are imprisoned within their own languages; the Captain's unrequited sexual fantasies suggest that he is trapped within what the sociologist Max Weber called the 'iron cages' of bourgeois life:

> CAPTAIN. Woyzeck, you have no virtue. You are not a
> virtuous man. Flesh and blood? When I'm lying by the
> window and it's been raining and I see the white
> stockings tripping down the alleyways – damn it,
> Woyzeck, I feel love! I too am flesh and blood. But
> Woyzeck, Virtue, Virtue!

The Captain is like a man in a fat suit, confined utterly by role – but giving intimations of the cost of wearing it.

In representing Woyzeck and his common-law wife Marie, Büchner adopts the existential approach of Euripides. By training his lens relentlessly on Woyzeck, he unpicks the tragic inevitability of his crime and the stereotyped attributes of criminality attributed to him by his elders and betters. Woyzeck is a philosopher, a social critic, a father (noting even how his son 'sweats in his sleep'), a barber, the object of an experiment, a cuckold and a murderer. By assembling a series of fragments in which these roles flash up and are displaced, Büchner shows human possibility, and how it can be extinguished. Even Marie is shown as a complicated character, repudiating and soliciting the advances of the Drum Major all at once. The tiny scene in which she is seduced is infamously hard to fathom; even within the space of a line Marie's reponses switch from 'Don't touch me!' to 'Oh who cares. It's all the same', reflecting Woyzeck's insight that 'Everyone is an abyss. You get dizzy if you look down'.

This bipolar approach to characterisation – where a character is composed of opposing traits – goes on to permeate twentieth-century plays. Brecht formalises and even dramatises the split personality in the characters of the Good Person of Setchuan and Herr Puntila. In expressionist drama, such as Sophie Treadwell's *Machinal*, the central character Helen Jones might be permitted an inner life but she is surrounded by malevolent types – doctors, lawyers, bosses, her mother, co-workers – all of whom speak in a dialogue reduced to machine-like cliché and act entirely according to type. In the plays of Lorca, Eliot, Beckett or Ionesco, character is rendered in the static mode of medieval archetype, or the music hall, or folk drama, but the world they inhabit is frighteningly real. In Sarah Kane's or Martin Crimp's plays, character again is not permitted complex expression and becomes a kind of willed cipher to some wider social process. In this, as in all matters, the history of plays may not be a linear one.

Character Function

Whilst characters often exceed their function, character nonetheless begins with function. So many plays never achieve lift-off because they are heavy with fascinating but superfluous people, duplicating each other's roles in the play without making problematic that duplication (a technique that drives *The Comedy of Errors*). For a playwright there's always a balloon debate to be carried out with one's characters – only the essential can be admitted, and any ballast must be ejected. It's a useful exercise with any play to lay your hand over the dramatis personae one by one in order to see what's lost from the story as each character is eliminated. Ibsen, whose plays carry in our terms a hefty but not enormous burden of parts, is actually, perhaps with the exception of *The Wild Duck*, ruthless with his characters. Look at *A Doll's House*:

NORA – Evidently indispensable to the plot as she *is* the plot, both our moral centre and the protagonist; without Nora there simply is no play.

TORVALD – As the primary antagonist he too is hardly expendable; he necessitates and blocks the core action and in his resistance to Nora's secret project he embodies the world of the Norwegian bourgeoisie.

KROGSTAD – It is possible that Krogstad might be heard of rather than seen, yet he usefully mirrors Torvald and reveals the seamier side of the offstage world of the bank; also the imminence of his threat deepens all the characters' dilemmas.

DR RANK – If we were to be crudely culling characters, Rank might be considered for such a fate; yet if we remove him from the drama, Nora has neither confidante nor hope, and we have no benchmark within the settled bourgeois against which to assess the predicament she is in.

MRS LINDE – Again a prime candidate for the blue pencil; yet without Linde's supplicatory mission to Nora it would be nigh impossible to extract the backstory of the play – and indeed she offers one rather bleak image of life beyond marriage.

In assessing the necessity of each of the characters, a task increasingly essential in a cash-strapped medium like the theatre, a number of different notions of function emerge:

Plot function

As structural analysts of stories from Vladimir Propp to A.J. Greimas have noted, there are archetypal roles in any tale – the donor, the hero, the villain, the false friend and so on. These basic functions may be fulfilled by different characters at different points in the play, but as functions they remain constant; they are the integers of the plot, necessary for things to happen. Theatre provides another filter, by asking which roles need to be actively present in the telling of the tale.

In *Oedipus Tyrannus* the roll-call of the story includes the Sphinx, Laius, Merope and so on. In the plot, figures such as the messenger, Tiresias and the old shepherd deputise for their function. If there is a primary way of determining function it must be plot.

Thematic function

Characters embody ideas and complicate the implicit meanings of the play; they frame and reflect each other, and indeed enable aspects of the protagonist to be illuminated: Mrs Linde is the only other woman besides the maid in Nora's play, and thus she is critical in revealing gender possibilities in the world of the play; Krogstad and Rank set Torvald in focus, enabling us to place him on a social spectrum and imagine different futures and pasts for him. Every onstage character stands in for all those who are absent, and to that extent they necessarily perform what we might call a 'choric' role.

Tonal function

It's useful to think of characters in a play as being equivalent to instruments in an orchestra – they bring with them colours, textures and effects. Ibsen's palette is deliberately restricted: Nora has a high woodwind quality modulating into a viola, set against Rank's fairly constant bassoon, Torvald's thudding strings and Mrs Linde's warning triangle, while Krogstad supplies the fate theme on the timpani. There's also a degree to which Rank brings a kind of pathetic social comedy, Torvald a modulation of farce with social realism, Mrs Linde Dickensian pathos, Krogstad thriller, and Nora comedy shifting to tragedy.

Character as Interaction

What's most critical about character is the impact each has on one another. Character does not exist in isolation; it's a mistake to try to replicate from the novel those extended, descriptive accounts of a character, and with good reason we tend to skip over those interpolations in Miller's or Shaw's stage directions – telling us what a character is in advance has no real value, for they are nothing until we see them revealed before us. The elements of a character's biography should be as portable as possible, only flashing up to serve the needs of the scene. To this end it is important for playwrights and directors to resist the desire of actors to excavate a total biography for their part; Pinter's famous retort to a question about the past of one of his characters – 'None of your damn business' – is apposite here. A spareness of authorial evocation of character in the dramatis personae best serves the necessary open-endedness of characterisation in plays – for different actors will bring very different attributes to any particular role.

Edward Bond's account of the characters in *Saved* shows that he conceived them in physical terms ('LEN, twenty-one. Tall, slim, firm, bony. Big hands. High, sharp cheekbones. Pleasant pale complexion – not ashen. Blue eyes, thick fair hair a bit oily, brushed sideways from a parting. Prominent feet'). Such prescriptions can hardly be slavishly obeyed; rather they show that in Bond's world psychology is secondary to the body. Miller's delineations often reveal his ethical concerns and desire to place character in social context, as with this account of Chris in *All My Sons*: 'He is thirty-two; like his father, solidly built, a listener. A man capable of immense affection and loyalty.' The hyper-vivid observations that often preface Tennessee Williams's plays are provocations rather than descriptions. There is in effect nothing to describe because nothing exists in advance of the action.

Given the interactive nature of theatrical characterisation, those exercises where writers list their character's favourite food, colour, hairstyle and happiest experience are beside the point. Planning a character in advance of the story only means it will be structured around peripheral quirks rather than core actions.

Consider *King Lear* again: in the opening scene we meet Gloucester and Kent, and Gloucester is auditing his two sons, drawing distinctions between them. This sets up our expectations about them, but perhaps we also feel that it is rather unfatherly and preferential behaviour – Kent certainly thinks so:

> KENT. Is not this your son, my lord?
>
> GLOUCESTER. His breeding, sir, hath been at my charge. I have so often blushed to acknowledge him that now I am brazed to't. [...] Do you smell a fault?
>
> KENT. I cannot wish the fault undone, the issue of it being so proper.

Who then is Kent? He is comprised of his response to Gloucester, and then, more tellingly, his later responses to Lear. Later in this scene, Kent's ability to say to his master 'See better, Lear', can only be understood in relation to the sum of the other characters' reactions to their monarch or father; after all, only he and Cordelia brook the King's will, and the reward for this resistance is instant banishment. We infer all sorts of things from his courage: not merely that he is courageous, but also that Lear's behaviour is new today, that this disregard for counsel is unprecedented, and finally that this King might therefore be worth the loyalty Kent goes on to exhibit.

Shakespeare could have written: 'Enter KENT, LEAR's forty-year-old and most trusted advisor; LEAR will tolerate from KENT what he would find inadmissible from anyone else; both men are grizzled from shared battles and indeed KENT's early role as his page cemented a relationship that moves from servitude to brotherly parity.' But he didn't, and nor did he need to, because all of this is implicit in the scattering of lines Kent offers in the scene, and the intemperate responses he receives. Similiarly, Cordelia, notoriously enigmatic, perhaps especially so to contemporary audiences, expresses her past relationship with Lear, her relative youth, her expectation of her father and her conception of truth in her simple word: 'Nothing.' The eloquence of her silence is the clearest conception of her character and that eloquence is derived from the noise that surrounds her.

Character Ecology

So much of the art of the dramatist lies in the creation of character. The degree to which characters and their predicaments burn into our memories determines the survival of the play – the uniqueness of Hamlet, Faustus and Mother Courage means they transcend their stories and become part of the wider human culture. The momentousness of their predicaments and the profundity of their desires lift the plays they inhabit out of their immediate context and into the collective imagination. This is apparent even when comparing characters within plays of comparable merit: Hedda Gabler has earned her eponymous status and astonishing longevity to a greater degree than Mrs Alving in

Ghosts. There are many analogies between them, yet Hedda's sheer intensity, the direness of the mismatch between her self-image and the world she finds herself in, and the relative moral danger she enters into compared to Mrs Alving, propels her into posterity. Mrs Alving's fate is dreadful and poignant, yet it is too late in the day and she is ultimately too circumscribed by role and theme to stand in relief from her play. However, the opposite impact also becomes apparent: Hedda is so vivid, so contemptuous and so clearly defined that, rather like Hamlet, she renders all other characters in her play secondary; they seem to inhabit quite a different genre. It's as if she has no predator and overwhelms her ecosystem like a piranha in a goldfish bowl. *Ghosts*, as its title suggests, is an ensemble piece, with Osvald, Manders and Mrs Alving all sharing the burden of the predicament between them; that is the character ecology dictated by that particular story.

Equally, compare *King Lear* with *Hamlet*: the former is in fact less character-driven than it at first suggests, largely because it takes place in a simpler, pre-Christian universe, but also because its concerns are distributed across the whole canvas of humanity into the natural world itself. Actors who make a meal of Lear endanger the character equilibrium elsewhere, and recent high-speed productions at the revived Shakespeare's Globe have revealed that this is not a play about psychology but a collective act of storytelling. In *King Lear*, hierarchy breaks down but it is ever present, and it is the means by which we read character against character and the frame by which we judge them – when it disappears altogether there is nothing but madness or barbarism. *Hamlet*, in contrast, is profoundly psychological; there would be no place for Hamlet's soliloquies in *Lear*, where solo speech is largely expository, the transcription of folk-madness, or simply the heightened expression of pain. This is not to do with craft (after all, *Lear* was written after *Hamlet*), and everything to do with the character ecology. Claudius is as psychologically complex and devious as Hamlet, if less ethically profound; the mystery that gathers around Gertrude is likewise suggestive of her refusal to be reduced to type. Essentially there is more to these characters than meets the eye, and that is what the play is about.

Creating Shapes for Actors

Characters are intrinsic to the appeal of a play, which conceals another insight – which is that *actors* are intrinsic to the appeal of a play. Shakespeare was a company man who wrote for specific actors, who wrote indeed to give work to these actors – a comic role for Will Kemp, a tragic one for Richard Burbage. Wilde courted actors from Lillie Langtry to Sarah Bernhardt through his characters. Brecht constructed Galileo around Charles Laughton's considerable girth.

For a playwright, the playability of a character, the scope it gives an actor, is a critical and not secondary consideration. This does not mean that writers should subscribe to the vanity of actors or the idea that all characters must be lovable (a gruesome heresy deriving from Hollywood); but the character who exists only to perform a single function, who is no more than a spear-carrier, is an indication of a writer disregarding the actor. The distribution of the writer's sympathies is a matter of craft and form. To invoke John Osborne again, *Look Back in Anger* seems to me an intolerable work because it's a narcissistic one – for all the power of Jimmy Porter's rhetoric, the deficit of imagination in the rendering of his victims (the poor hapless Cliff and the benighted Alison) make the play formally and politically limited, and lock it within the time of its writing, as a testimony to the constipated self-pity of lower-middle-class masculinity. Likewise, *The Entertainer* leaves so little for actors condemned to play the subaltern roles of Archie Rice's family. This cannot be said of the fellow-travellers in Nora Helmer's drama of liberation – Torvald is a great and complex creation, funny and exasperating by turns, just as Dr Rank is an indelibly rich role to play. They are parts no actor would shun.

There is a deeper issue concerning the choices writers make in creating roles; one that derives from their relationship to the wider world and the audience itself. The expansion through time of the range of social classes represented on the stage reflects nothing less than the ongoing extension of power to the unrepresented. Through actors, writers work to extend the audience's ambit of sympathy. Plays in which working-class characters are limited to the role of servants without apparent inner life were rendered anachronistic by *Woyzeck*; *A Doll's House* and *Top Girls* made laughable the invidious presumption that women exist only to meet the reductive needs of men. After the plays of August Wilson, Kwame Kwei-Armah, Tanika Gupta and Ayub Khan-Din, there can be no return to an exclusively white stage that imagines itself a complete portrait of the world, just as Tony Kushner, Joe Orton and Bryony Lavery have ensured that gay identity can no longer be represented solely through theatrical euphemism. This set of invocations could continue, but while it is apparently a political roll-call it in fact has deep implications for dramatic art and characterisation. All these writers ultimately sought to create great roles, roles which reverberate with the changing and enduring nature of the audience, roles which create shapes for newly conceived identities. Sometimes this is simply a question of numbers – more female roles, more non-white roles. But more profoundly it is about the complexity of those roles, and their resonance. Martin Crimp's instruction at the beginning of his *Attempts on her Life*, that the play should be performed by a company of actors 'whose composition should reflect the composition of the world beyond the theatre', is a telling prescription; for often the spur to writing a play is the recognition of an inadequacy in existing representations of people on the stage, and the dream of the theatre continues to be one of a democracy of representation that goes way beyond the existing forms outside it.

Chapter Six
Powers of Speech: Language as Rhetoric

The astonishing linguistic fullness of Shakespeare can be dispiriting for a contemporary dramatist. How could one brain bring forth so many levels of language, so many stratagems for expressing feeling, such density of words and allusion? The palette of the modern playwright seems to lack ninety per cent of those colours and potentialities, despite the expansion of English in the interim between Shakespeare and us. Is the language of the contemporary stage condemned to be a bloodless echo of that plenitude?

This is partially a trick of time. In fact, since Shakespeare's time the ongoing incorporation of argots and dialects and lexicons into English has unleashed incredible verbal riches in playwriting, a process that is far from over. From Howard Barker's *The Castle* to Enda Walsh's *Disco Pigs* through to debbie tucker green's *stoning mary*, from ntozake shange's *for colored girls who have considered suicide when the rainbow is enuf* to Steven Berkoff's *East*, plays continue to be powered by sheer linguistic brio.

Yet it's instructive to recall just how profoundly rooted Shakespeare's stage and world was in the spoken word; how the high-octane language of his plays and those of his contemporaries rested upon a grammar-school system committed to oratory; and how central to that was the notion of rhetoric. For there is a philistinism inherent in a lot of academic and theatrical criticism, which seems word-blind, insensitive to the centrality of words to plays, positing indeed that words should come last, whereas so often for writers they come first.

Too often we accept this notion that words are secondary rather than primary in the theatrical lexicon. When great directors such as Peter Brook seek to excavate 'a language beyond words' for the stage, where a whole movement dubs itself 'physical theatre' to avoid association with the 'literary' stage, the inherent dynamism of words, and by extension rhetoric, is too often overlooked.

At his grammar school in Stratford, Shakespeare learned to debate *in utramque partem*, arguing against positions of consensus, and thereby to think dialectically in the manner of the Humanist scholar Erasmus, with his book-length praise of folly. He learned the particle-fine declinations of language inherited from classical rhetoric, absorbing terms and conceits, such as the following:

Accumulatio – Piling up praise or blame to clinch an argument.

Apophasis – Feigning denial in order to affirm.

Apoplanesis – Using digression to evade an issue.

These three terms already conjure into being a character, a Polonius or a Holofernes or any one of Shakespeare's deadly pedants. Polonius's declaration of Hamlet's madness in Act Two, Scene Two fuses *accumulatio* and *apoplanesis*:

> My liege, and madam, to expostulate
> What majesty should be, what duty is,
> Why day is day, night night, and time is time,
> Were nothing but to waste night, day and time.
> Therefore, since brevity is the soul of wit
> And tediousness the limbs and outward flourishes,
> I will be brief. Your noble son is mad.

This hilarious mixture of tactlessness and pomposity derives from Shakespeare's ear and relish for rhetoric's absurdity and its power. That lost knowledge he was intimate with, generated by classical authorities such as Horace or Quintilius, offered verbal stratagems to the great orators of Rome. But what it concerns itself with is the power of language to persuade, rather than literary priorities of linguistic burnish. It is a muscular sort of knowledge highly pertinent to dramatists, who are primarily shapers of playable speech, artificers of language seeking to make words move both actors and audiences.

It's hardly desirable to restore a world of homilies, sermons, public addresses, and high formality. I'm not proposing that aspiring playwrights should have rhetorical terms drummed into them. Yet all playwrights think deeply about language and its functioning, and this chapter attempts to offer some clarifying observations about the forms of linguistic power observable in life and plays, and to draw upon the work of linguists in doing so. Rhetoric is key to this. Brecht, a great poet as well as dramatist, speaks of the gestural quality of language and his aim to achieve a language to show 'human dealings as contradictory, fiercely fought over, full of violence'. To that end he sought a 'gestic' mode, syncopated, irregular, but rhythmic and expressive. His insight holds good for all dramatic language, which is full of implicit gestures, actions caught in words. To consider language rhetorically, in the manner director Max Stafford-Clark considers it, that is transitively, is a crucial distinction between the language of plays and inert verbiage. For the transitive nature of language in plays is apparent in speech's movement from speaker to listener, in dialogue's transactional quality. Polonius's fancy, self-admiring speech is verbose but it's not 'inert': he deploys his colours of rhetoric to dazzle, to evade, and to mystify his hearers; the verbiage is a stratagem of character, and for this reason the words don't play in a heavy, literary fashion. Likewise, Shakespeare is not demonstrating his own linguistic finesse as an end in itself, but as a form of active portraiture, making Polonius instantly present through language.

Register; or Worlds of Language

Sociolinguists are interested in genres of language, and so are playwrights. As we travel through the world, we travel through worlds of language, or what Wittgenstein called 'language games', all with their own internal rules and functioning. Often the power dynamic within a play derives from the battle for supremacy between idioms; one of the tasks of the dramatist is to test each idiom to its limits, to audit their truthfulness or evasiveness. Martin Crimp, probably the most accomplished anatomist of language currently writing, begins *Attempts on her Life* with a kind of overture of the language games within the play: globalisation ('I'm calling from Vienna'), art-crit-speak ('Let's just say the trees have names'), terrorism ('You leave the device in a small truck...'), sales ('This is Sally at Cooper's'), porn ('Let me tell you what I am going to do to you'), and so on. Each register conjures up a distinctive personality and world.

The terrifying lesson of Crimp's play is that character is dictated by register, that self is a construct of social being. The message beginning 'This is Sally at Cooper's' ushers in a world of brightness, blandness, the assumed camaraderie inherent in modern consumerism; just as Ionesco revealed in his *The Bald Prima Donna* that merely placing the uninflected words of an English phrase book in the mouths of actors creates hilarity. Then the pornographic message ('Good evening Anne. Let me tell you what I am going to do to you. First you're going to suck my cock'), with its insouciant, coercive formality, crystallises another way of being, in sharp comic contrast to Sally at Cooper's, and rendering the listener more confused as to who Anne might be.

Crimp also demonstrates in his fragments of register how quickly the inherent gesture of language reveals a world. By addressing Anne as 'Annie', a later message instantly sets up the fuzzy, evangelically inspired sentiment that follows ('It's quarter after ten here in Minnesota...'). The next caller ('Anne? Brilliant. It's moving. It's timely. It's distressing...'), with their lack of formality, stream of contradictory adjectives, and high-speed sentences, suggestive of a trendy art critic, implicates the listener in the character's smug cleverness and urbanity. Crimp's messages demonstrate how language so often confers a role through terms of address, implied shared knowledge and codes the listener is assumed to be privy to.

Our capacity to recognise a register is sufficiently well-acquired and fine-tuned to admit of such swift conjurations. In a sense, our degree of socialisation depends on our acquisition of the most extensive range of registers possible: formal educational, informal subcultural, familial informal, professional formal. Even within a professional territory registers proliferate – take the theatre: technicians talk of 'cheating' the lights and of PAT-testing, the designer of 'palettes' and scenography, the box office of 'walk-ups' and 'capacity houses', the director of 'front-foot lines' and 'speed-runs', the literary manager of 'dramaturgical interventions', the education team of 'wraparound learning', and so on. Professional jargon of this kind can be both inclusive (we share this trade) and exclusive (you don't share this trade) but, as with all terminology, the speaker is compelled to perform their own proficiency by playing the role implicit in the register, indicating they can crack the code and talk the talk.

The following checklist offers a way of analysing register in action:

Formal/informal
Context is crucial to the way in which any language game operates; in public contexts (for instance, legal settings), the encoded protocol of register apportions 'speaking rights': implied rules in language as to who may speak and when, as well as what content is 'inadmissable'. Yet informality too can be as rule-bound as formality – the judge who speaks to her husband in the cautious legalese of the day job would transgress that implicit rule pretty swiftly. The fact that these codes are rarely defined is intentional, making it easy to transgress them, and thereby reveal yourself as an outsider.

Specialised vocabulary
With the register comes a code or a jargon which forms a kind of shibboleth to distinguish between insiders and outsiders. Often the terms may not be capable of outside definition – think of subcultural words such as 'hip' or 'cool' which function in this way, or inversions ('That is so *bad*'); the words chosen don't so much refer to real referents as reflect back on the speaker.

Implicit roles
Every register brings with it a ready-made map of power. Think of the way terms of address work within each one: in court ('Your Honour', 'The Accused'), politics ('The Honourable Member', 'Mr President'), the street ('Blood', 'Cheers, buddy').

Each form of address posits a relationship of equality or implied subjection. As English has moved away from explicit distinctions of rank evident in pronouns such as 'You' and 'Thou', registers have accumulated in more coded forms.

If success in life often stems from the mastery of the widest spectrum of registers, so in the richest plays dramatists pit the most comprehensively realised worlds of language against one other. Caryl Churchill's chameleon-like progress through the dominant registers of present and past accounts for her remarkable longevity and freshness as a dramatist. To take a sample of her work:

Cloud Nine – highly formalised registers of nineteenth-century imperialism and household relations set against the informal registers of sexual liberation.

Light Shining in Buckinghamshire – registers of formal Parliamentarianism set against the egalitarian registers of dissenters and ranters.

Top Girls – a polyphony of historical registers (early theology, travel discourse, Japanese Court) set against Thatcherite corporate speech and the inarticulacy of East Anglian deprivation.

Fen – the sociolect of a female rural workforce set against corporate speech and intense dissenting religiosity.

Serious Money – registers of new corporate finance set against a more formal, hidebound City voice.

Churchill continues to explore new registers in her work; what's remarkable is that each new play demonstrates an under-standing of some underlying conflict within language, inflected by Churchill's own unmistakable voice. Her serial competencies in all these idioms reveal the way in which playwriting serves to place under the microscope the dominant languages of the day, expressing and challenging Wittgenstein's aphorism that 'the limits of my language are the limits of my world'.

While dialogue in plays can be considered as a kind of transaction between characters, it can also be looked at in terms of what it tells us about an individual character:

Idiolect – The specific language of an individual character, formed out of the stew of influences that have shaped him or her. A useful example is Othello, whose grandiose rhetoric is a rich soup of exoticism, bombast and militarism.

Sociolect – A character's voice is shaped by and representative of a class or profession or way of life: whether they are urban or rural, whether they derive from a highly repressed and formal culture (a religious sect, for example), or a rougher, looser one.

Dialect – The geographical context that shapes the character also dictates their language; and indeed dialect has often been so particular as to overwhelm other layers of language.

A character's struggle is so often to exist between and beyond these levels of language. Think of Woyzeck trying to shape his own idiolect from fragments of proverbs, the Bible, via the dialect of his native Darmstadt-Hesse, set against the Doctor's sociolect of abstract natural science:

> DOCTOR. Woyzeck, you have the finest *aberratio mentalis partialis* of the second category, quite pronounced.

Or when Angie in *Top Girls* makes a surprise visit to her 'aunt' Marlene in her London office and witnesses her magnificently brutal dismissal of Mrs Kidd – here Churchill captures the poignant contrast between Angie's heartfelt, slightly childlike idiolect (combined with the bluntness of her Suffolk dialect) and her mother's breezy, detached corporate sociolect:

> MARLENE. I've got to go and do some work now. Will you come back later?
>
> ANGIE. I think you were wonderful.
>
> MARLENE. I've got to go and do some work now.
>
> ANGIE. You told her to piss off.
>
> MARLENE. Will you come back later?
>
> ANGIE. Can't I stay here?
>
> MARLENE. Don't you want to go sightseeing?

ANGIE. I'd rather stay here.

MARLENE. You can stay here I suppose, if it's not boring.

ANGIE. It's where I most want to be in the world.

Pinter's great game in so many of his plays is to grant a character competence in an unexpected register or sociolect: Lenny in *The Homecoming* suddenly outflanking his academic brother Teddy in the register of logical positivism, or Goldberg in *The Birthday Party* turning on Stanley with a sophisticated language game:

GOLDBERG. Is the number 846 possible or necessary?

STANLEY. Neither.

GOLDBERG. Wrong! Is the number 846 possible or necessary?

STANLEY. Both.

GOLDBERG. Wrong! It's necessary but not possible.

STANLEY. Both.

GOLDBERG. Wrong! Why do you think the number 846 is necessarily impossible?

Pinter's plays track the way contemporary languages and registers can be turned against each other. In *The Caretaker*, he manages to make the banal register of interior decorating at once sinister and comic, as Mick 'ruminates' on improving the junk-strewn attic that the tramp Davies wishes to make his own:

MICK. [...] I could turn this place into a penthouse. For instance... this room. This room you could have as the kitchen. [...] I'd have... I'd have teal-blue, copper and parchment linoleum squares. I'd have those colours re-echoed in the walls. I'd offset the kitchen units with charcoal-grey worktops. [...] it wouldn't be a flat it'd would be a palace.

DAVIES. I'd say it would, man.

MICK. A palace.

DAVIES. Who would live there?

MICK. I would. My brother and me.

Pause.

DAVIES. What about me?

Mick has hitherto said little, largely forming a figure of menace in the background, so this sudden lyrical vision is strangely shocking – not least because every one of his leisurely, itemised and kitschy proposals is in fact a veiled threat to Davies, for whom this serves as a notice of eviction.

Articulate Inarticulacy

Audiences naturally distrust characters who are too proficient in language; all too often articulacy plays as glibness. Largely this stems from our sense that at points of intensity and emotion the intellect gives way to something more primary; if the language does not mirror this, the moment rings false. This suspicion has certainly placed so much of the work of a dramatist such as Shaw under question; the great success of *Saint Joan* derives from those moments where Joan interrupts the flow of words with sudden apostrophes and cries – the shocked silence at the Court's final, cruel verdict on her or the incapability of an onlooker to describe her unspeakable offstage burning. Such moments admit something beyond the intellect onto the stage. Let's not forget that Shaw's reputation was sealed by the phrase 'Not bloody likely' in *Pygmalion*, rather than the torrent of cleverness surrounding it.

In most playwriting there is an anti-rhetoric that works in counterpoint with linguistic potency and grounds it, and that comes from the fact that speech and thought do not always run in step. The greatest lines in *King Lear*, for instance, enact Lear fighting to make sense and failing, from 'I shall do such things, what they are I know not yet but they will be the terrors of the earth' to 'Nothing nothing nothing nothing'. Shakespeare's artful inarticulacies create a space for feeling to emerge. Indeed, linguists helpfully identify how seemingly incommunicative matter in everyday speech serves to frame and energise moments of articulacy.

Redundancy

Whilst this term sounds pejorative in the context of playwriting, it in fact touches upon an area crucial to the functioning of dramatic language as oral language – that is, that speech is full of semantic waste, what we might call 'fillers', as the speaker prepares for their next thought to take shape, attempting to stay 'live' in language as they do. Take the opening of Bond's *Saved*, where Len and Pam become acquainted in Pam's living room:

LEN. This ain' the bedroom.

PAM. Bed ain' made.

LEN. Oo's bothered?

PAM. It's awful. 'Ere's nice.

LEN. Suit yourself. Yer don't mind if I take me shoes off?
 (*He kicks them off.*) No one 'ome?

PAM. No.

LEN. Live on your tod?

PAM. No.

LEN. O.

 Pause. He sits back on the couch.

 Yer all right? Come over 'ere.

PAM. In a minit.

LEN. Wass your name?

PAM. Yer ain' arf nosey.

LEN. Somethin' up?

PAM. Can't I blow me nose?

The direct communicative content of this extract could be expressed far more pithily and in significantly less stage time. But Bond reveals the way in which speech serves its own purpose; the rhetorical questions ('Oo's bothered?', Len's perfunctory civility about his shoes, Pam and her nose), the tag phrases ('Suit yourself', 'In a minit'), the non sequiturs ('Somethin' up?' / 'Can't I blow me nose?'), the repetitions ('No one 'ome?' / 'No.' / 'Live on your tod?' / 'No.') all reveal his patterned use of the redundancy of ordinary speech. Partially this functions as an element of the play's realism (conjuring up a taciturn world), partially it serves a rhythmic purpose (the ebb and flow of Len's rebuffed questions). But the sheer superfluity of speech over action directs us to its other function beyond ostensible communication, that of 'phatic' utterance, the desire for the character to signal their presence in language.

Turn-taking

The distribution of language between speakers and the way in which dialogue is an enactment of group identity is another crucial aspect of language behaviour. Look at how turn-taking operates in a scene and its implicit power-map is laid bare. We start learning such tacit protocols of speech from the moment we first observe our parents in dialogue: when to speak and when to stop, how to enter into speech and how to exit, the acts of framing and reframing that underlie all intercourse. In Scene Six of *Saved*, as the gang of men bears down on the unfortunate baby in the pram, Bond makes their turn-taking seamless:

> COLIN. Look at that mouth.
>
> BARRY. Flippin' yawn.
>
> PETE. Least it's tryin'.
>
> MIKE. Pull its drawers off.
>
> COLIN. Yeh!
>
> MIKE. Less case its ol' crutch.
>
> PETE. Ha!
>
> BARRY. Yeh!
>
> > *He throws the nappy in the air.*
> >
> > Yippee!
>
> COLIN. Look at that!

There are five men present: Fred, the baby's father, looks on non-committal as yet; when he joins in, the baby's fate is sealed. What makes the scene so disturbing is Bond's careful plotting of complicity as the smooth and inexorable turn-taking lures the group into the atrocity.

Silence

There has been more ink spilled on the subject of silence than on any other aspect of modern drama, so I won't dwell on it here except to note its relative rarity in ordinary speech. Indeed, when speech fails in ordinary interaction a crisis of some magnitude has occurred. Of course, within families a companionable or sullen silence might be the normal course of affairs, but within other interactions silence signals the failure of the participants to generate utterance – a rule has been broken, a role refused. As a consequence, playwrights have become rather profligate with it, scattering pauses like ordinary items of punctuation and forgetting the danger silence represents. Pinter, in conversation with Mel Gussow, commented in a usefully demystifying fashion on the fetishisation of the pause:

> From my point of view [pauses and silences] are not in any sense a formal kind of arrangement. The pause is a pause because of what has just happened in the minds and guts of the characters. They spring out of the text. They're not formal conveniences or stresses... a silence equally means that something has happened to create the impossibility of anyone speaking for a certain amount of time.

The real question is why any character ceases to speak and why any character chooses to respond. In that respect the full stop is as significant as the pause, which after all is a rupture in the smooth progression of turn-taking that any successful act of speech aspires to. Silence is mortifying, as is apparent in the heartbreaking scene between Varya and Lopakhin in *The Cherry Orchard*, within which a long-anticipated proposal of marriage is expected to finally emerge:

> *A pause. Offstage, a stifled laugh and whispering,* VARYA *finally enters.*
>
> VARYA (*inspects the luggage at some length*). That's strange, I can't find it anywhere...
>
> LOPAKHIN. What are you looking for?
>
> VARYA. I packed these myself, and now I can't remember.
>
> *A pause.*
>
> LOPAKHIN. So where are you off to now, Miss Varvara?
>
> VARYA. Me? I'm going to the Ragulins'... I've agreed to look after the house for them... I'll be a sort of housekeeper.
>
> LOPAKHIN. And that's at Yashnevo? That'll be about fifty miles from here.
>
> *A pause.*
>
> So life in this house is over now.
>
> VARYA (*examining the luggage*). Where on earth is it...? Maybe I packed it away in the trunk... Yes, life's finished in this house... there'll be nothing left...

The power of this scene stems from the mutual refusal or incapacity of its characters to switch from the register of professional formality into one of personal informality: Lopakhin refuses to engage in the expected language game of the proposal, and through his evasion the humiliation of Varya deepens (after all, this is conspicuously not a private scene, with the mortifying sense of onlookers giggling offstage). So the pauses, which elsewhere in the play and throughout Chekhov's work tend to suggest not so much turmoil as cogitation, here seem to imply Varya's expectation. She initiates the first pause by abandoning her feeble ruse of searching her luggage and silently passes the initiative to Lopakhin. She's also responsible for the second one, by not permitting Lopakhin a release from the implicit role the scene demands of him and ignoring his digressive question about Yashnevo. As with all authentic silences, the impact on the audience is a profound unease, as if the show itself has come to some impasse. The trailing-off, the non sequiturs, the unanswered questions all combine to create an undercurrent of unrequited feeling and evasion which is mutely eloquent.

Linguistic Energy

Immediacy is the aim of all dramatic speech, and language carries within it potential energy as well as opposing forces of inertia. The effective dramatist deploys the latter as displaced energy and not out of their own sluggishness of expression. For, as the playwright Howard Brenton has said of Brecht, language in the theatre has to be fast in its workings, and the primary characteristics of good, vigorous theatrical language are wit and attack. If an image or idea is clumsy and laborious, it will defuse the play's inner energy.

What are the enemies of language's potential energy, the deadening forces?

Past tense

'Do you remember?' are the three deadliest words in the English language for playwrights. If the past tense is allowed to predominate, urgency is lost. Martin Crimp's *The Country* begins with blinding urgency even though it pivots on a past event, that of Richard bringing a woman into the family home:

- Because why did you bring her here? Why ever did you bring her here?
- It's my job to bring her here.
- What? Into our house? In the middle of the night?
- Yes.
- Is it?
- Yes.
- Your *job*? It's your job to bring a strange woman into our house in the middle of the night?
- As I understand it.

After the first line, everything is in the present tense of confrontation. The more the events that precede the play are contested in the present, the more active they become; exposition is thereby turned into action.

Description

Depending on the tense, description is either exposition at its most undisguised or rendered superfluous by the visible reality of the scene. Let loose, it imports the unhurried aspect of the novel into a scene and brings the narrative to a halt. Only when description is an action rather than an evocation does it serve the play; any description that is not dramatically motivated hangs in the air like fog. When Hamlet vividly contrasts his dead father with Claudius, it is no mere exercise of linguistic prowess:

> Look here upon this picture, and on this,
> The counterfeit presentment of two brothers.
> See what a grace was seated on this brow;
> Hyperion's curls, the front of Jove himself,
> [...]
>
> This was your husband. Look you now what follows.
> Here is your husband, like a mildewed ear
> Blasting his wholesome brother. Have you eyes?

The classical allusions and hyperbole devoted to his dead father are not so much description as Hamlet inflaming himself – the deification sets up the vitriolic attack on Claudius, and the precision of 'mildewed' against 'wholesome' offers the actor a vehicle to embody physically Hamlet's repulsion. The startling physical specificity delineates the obsessive quality of his mental state. Likewise, when Anna (the ghostly guest at Kate and Deeley's house in *Old Times*) offers a lengthy description of the park, it is with the purpose of dissuading Kate from crossing it:

> The park is dirty at night, all sorts of horrible people, men hiding behind trees and women with terrible voices, they scream at you as you go past, and people come out suddenly from behind trees and bushes and there are shadows everywhere and there are policeman, and you'll have a horrible walk...

The act of describing the park is so luridly done, and so charged by the playful act of dissuasion, that the accumulation of details doesn't diminish the scene's energy, but rather creates a further comic momentum.

Adjectives

'Sit at the formica table and eat the freshly-cooked spaghetti.' A bore is conjured instantly into life. Adjectives function only as a kind of rebuke. In *Old Times*, Deeley self-consciously plays with adjectives as another way of enacting his rivalry with Anna, of demonstrating his control over the past; so he describes himself to his wife as a former suitor of Anna: 'Of course I was slim-hipped in those days. Pretty nifty. A bit squinky, quite honestly. Curly hair. The lot.' The disembodied adjectives represent him claiming more and more control over past events.

Cliché

'I've waited all my life for this moment.' The second-hand, when not used consciously against itself, condemns a character to inauthenticity. Deeley is acutely conscious of this, and deploys cliché almost as a way of distancing himself from the situation he finds himself in, as when he brings in a cup of coffee to Anna at the opening of Act Two: 'Here we are. Good and hot. Good and strong and hot.' That repetition of the clichéd homeliness of a host removes the unaffected generosity of the first utterance and charges it with irony. Likewise, the 'Goodnight mother' of Hamlet dragging Polonius's cadaver brings a banal utterance to life precisely because it is so at odds with the context in which it is spoken.

This is an impertinent list. Yet it highlights the necessity of a present-focused language for the stage. How then is urgency created?

The imperative mode
Every imperative brings into the scene an urgency of task, and indeed reveals the distribution of power. Take the Captain's ceaseless ordering about of Woyzeck: 'Slowly, Woyzeck, slowly, one thing at a time... Pace yourself, Woyzeck... Keep busy... Say something... don't run so!' The energy inherent in imperatives brings us into the immediate moment where power is exercised.

Deixis
Playwrights, like poets, deploy 'pointing' words which situate us in space and time – this, that, here, there. The potency of such words lies in their particularity to the moment in which they are uttered: the present situation gives them meaning. Think of Lear's desperately sad last lines:

> Pray you, undo *this* button; thank you, Sir.
> Do you see *this*? Look on her; look, her lips,
> Look *there*, look *there*!

Imperatives abound, leading to implicit action; but the 'this' and 'there' create a spatially embodied quality to the moment too, because they direct us to that particular button, those particular lips.

Parataxis
That is, lists:

> Anyway, when we got to Paris it was cold there too, snowing. My French is abysmal. Mama was staying on the fourth floor, and when I went to see her she had all these French gentlemen with her, and ladies, and some old Catholic priest with his little book, and the whole place was full of tobacco smoke, very uncomfortable. I suddenly felt so sorry for Mama, so terribly sorry, that I put my

arms round her, pressed her head to my breast, and
couldn't let go. And Mama couldn't stop hugging and
kissing me, and crying…

Anya's account of her time in Paris in *The Cherry Orchard* is
active and dynamic because she seems to be processing it and
rendering it sensible for the first time here. The paratactic syntax ('and… and… and') is far from organised; it has an
improvisatory quality that, although rendering only a partial
description, is highly expressive and emotive as her memories
come tumbling out in a torrent of detail.

Punctuation and typography

Does a character end their speech with a dash or an ellipsis?
The former kind thinks in spurts and tears away from their
thoughts; the latter lets their thoughts peter out or loses faith
in them in the moment of utterance. Woyzeck is a man of
dashes, the Captain one of ellipses. David Mamet's characters
have a passion for parentheses and brackets, which indicate
their highly specified acts of speech, their passion for elucida-
tion; the speaker who litters their utterance with implied
colons is long-winded and out to fox you; whilst the exclama-
tion mark is rather taboo in modern theatre as it seems to
compensate for a lack of energy in the line. As for *italics* or CAP-
ITALISATION, they suggest a desire for emphasis that supersedes
the normative; an excess of them and the scene is a battle-
ground of storm and stress. Likewise from ee cummings to
ntozake shange and debbie tucker green, avoiding upper case,
or indeed conventional punctuation altogether, is a kind of
protest against the confines of standard English. Berkoff,
shange and others find their own system of punctuation
rooted in units of breath and governed by non-hierarchical
slashes.

Active verbs

The transitive verb is a conduit and vessel for energy. In its
imperative mode it galvanises the moment with futurity, with
impending action; active verbs generally carry within them the
promise of energy and movement. When Hamlet at the close
of Act Two imagines the impact of the Player King were he to

have 'the motive and the cue for passion / That I have...', he emphasises his imputed power through a torrent of active verbs:

> He would *drown* the stage with tears,
> And *cleave* the general ear with horrid speech,
> *Make mad* the guilty and *appal* the free,
> *Confound* the ignorant, and *amaze* indeed
> The very faculty of eyes and ears.

In the light of this, the weak, singular verb he attributes to himself ('Yet I... can say nothing') is eloquently intransitive and negative in effect.

Performative utterances

Since J.L. Austin's highly influential *How to Do Things with Words*, there's been a heightened awareness of the fact that language is often in itself a kind of event or action. Austin noted that certain acts of speech in particular contexts have the power to change the world: 'With this ring I thee wed', 'I hereby promise to repay the sum below by 2008', 'I swear it was him', 'I name you "Sir Peter"' – all these actions in the appropriate context bring new situations into being, commit the speaker in time and are a form of language in its irreversible mode. Such utterances as gestures get to the source of language power in plays, and it is the dramatist's task to uncover the most active language, where commitments, promises or curses unleash consequences. *King Lear* again provides rich examples of this: the first scene is littered with speech acts or performative utterance, from the division of the kingdom to the pronouncements of exile. The pathos and power of the later stages of the play derive from Lear's incapacity to 'do things with words'. From the conjurations in *Doctor Faustus* to Angie's proclamation that she's going to kill her mother in *Top Girls*, plays become dynamic when words become deeds. Claudius exemplifies this power in the second scene of *Hamlet* as he sends his diplomats to Norway ('...we here dispatch / You, good Cornelius, and you, Voltemand, / For bearers of this greeting to old Norway') then later grants Laertes's wish to go to Paris ('Take thy fair hour Laertes, time be thine / And thy best graces spend it at thy will'); as opposed to his subtle, cynical prevention of Hamlet's plans to leave ('Be as ourself in Denmark'). Camouflaged in the thickets of rhetoric, Claudius's steely soul emerges in his decisive speech acts.

Language at the Speed of Thought

A character can be measured by the velocity with which their thoughts convert to speech – do they blurt or do they ponder? A blurter is full of dramatic life and risk, but may appear giddy and reckless; a ponderer might be cautious and dull, or grounded and wise. The readiness to speak and the unfinished nature of thought in speech dictates how a character plays, as it often functions as an index of their inherent generosity, their aliveness.

This can accord with the aesthetic of the dramatist. Wilde's characters rarely blurt, which accounts for the polish and urbanity of the plays; epigrammatic lines such as his suggest a world where thought enters fully formed into speech, where all are subject to a kind of writerly decorum. As a consequence the plays tend to proceed at a fastidious, stately tempo and are cool in tenor even if hot feelings inform the aphorisms. Chekhov's characters, in contrast, are serial blurters whose speech forms a kind of adventure in language, often taking them to places they clearly did not envisage in advance; this is often attributed to their 'Russianness', as if Slavs had a monopoly on feeling. Yet Chekhov's notion of dialogue has had the more enduring influence because it permits the fullest psychological fluency; it lays bare the workings of thought in such an unprecedented manner.

Look at Lopakhin's opening speech in *The Cherry Orchard* as he stands with Dunyasha waiting for Madame Ranevskaya's return:

> Madame Ranevskaya's lived abroad for five years now, I've no idea what she'll be like... She's a fine woman. Straightforward, easy-going. I remember when I was a lad of about fifteen, my late father – he had a little shop in the village at that time – well, he hit me with his fist so hard my nose started bleeding. We'd come up here to the yard for something or other, and he'd been drinking. Anyway, Madame Ranevskaya – I remember even now – she was

just a slip of a girl, she took me over to the washbasin in this very room, in the nursery, 'Now don't cry, little peasant,' she said, 'It'll heal up in time for your wedding.'

A pause.

'Little peasant'... Well, true enough, my father was a peasant, but here I am now in a white waistcoat, and tan leather shoes. A silk purse out of a sow's ear, you might say. Plain fact is I'm rich, I've pots of money, but when you get right down to it, I'm a peasant through and through. (*Leafs through the book.*) Yes, I was reading this book, didn't understand a word. Fell asleep reading.

This remarkable speech is psychologically informed writing at its most acute. Firstly and crucially, eighteen years before Joyce writes *Ulysses* or Woolf *Mrs Dalloway*, Chekhov achieves, almost unremarked, the technique of stream of consciousness they became famous for. The journeying into thought and the getting lost there are wonderfully enacted in the very structure of the speech; the occasion of this eruption of memory (and it feels uncalculated) is meticulously engineered. Lopakhin is in a sense alone, though in the presence of Dunyasha, who is clearly hardly listening to his meditations, and this frees him from his habitual inhibitions; after all, she's not his servant. Also, the congruence of present anticipation (the imminent return of Ranevskaya) and past event (the encounter in the nursery) permits a concreteness of recollection comparable to those rushes of memory in the novels of Chekhov's contemporary Proust – the slip on the step in Venice, the dunked Madeleine, the smell of hawthorn.

But even in translation, the way verbalisation enacts internal recollection is startlingly vivid. Partly that's to do with Chekhov's depiction of the irregularity of remembrance. Lopakhin is caught between internal reverie and public explanation as he retreats into the past, and this makes the act of recollection tortuous. Firstly, he contemplates Ranevksaya, noting her five-year exile, which triggers apprehensions of change ('I've no idea what she'll be like...'); these revealing anxieties are hurriedly cancelled out by male bravado ('She's a fine woman'), her attributes ('Straightforward, easy-going') listed in an isolated sentence, suggestive of an afterthought of diminished conviction. Now erupts the speech's core memory, which ushers in a new momentum. Chekhov allows the past to ambush Lopakhin with its vividness, revealing an experience that for the character still retains its original shock. As he recalls his nosebleed, a rush of detail renders that moment overwhelming. Then the memory's real significance surfaces, as he recalls Ranevskaya's patronising consolation. In the pause that follows, his hopes to impress her crumble, with her past judgement ('Little peasant') provoking in him even now self-consciousness, and ultimately self-loathing.

So Lopakhin's entire trajectory is revealed in less than a page of dialogue. The speech is dynamic because it enacts so precisely the fluctuations of his feelings, the shifts between inward reflection and outer expression. There's nothing calculating in this unprecedented demonstration of the link between thought and language. Chekhov deploys fully expressed and fully formed sentences, then verbless ones, then sentences that peter out in mid-flow; ones interrupted by sudden dashes where self-consciousness intrudes; moments of precision jostle with moments of vagueness ('for something or other...'); cliché ('just a slip of a girl') with fresh-minted observation. What we see is the struggle to think, the way in which thought turns back on itself.

This of course is 'experience recollected in tranquility'. The other way in which the quick energies of thought and speech are represented comes mainly through dialogue that carries within it the improvisational energies of everyday speech. Different intensities of dialogue allow varying degrees of reflection to interrupt the progress from thought to speech. Arguments, one of the most challenging forms of dialogue, almost completely close the gap between the two.

One of the most innovative representations of an argument forms the opening of Ben Jonson's *The Alchemist*, where Face and Subtle come on in the midst of a real spat, with Dol Common vainly trying to mediate:

> *Enter* FACE (*with a sword*), SUBTLE (*with a phial*), DOL COMMON.
>
> FACE. Believe't, I will.
>
> SUBTLE.   Thy worst. I fart at thee.

DOL. Ha' you your wits? Why gentlemen! For love –

FACE. Sirrah, I'll strip you –

SUBTLE.   What to do? Lick figs
   Out at my –

FACE.   Rogue, rogue, out of all your sleights.

DOL. Nay, look ye! Sovereign, General, are you madmen?

SUBTLE. O, let the wild sheep loose. I'll gum your silks
   With good strong water, an' you come.

DOL.   Will you have
   The neighbours hear you? Will you betray all?
   Hark, I hear somebody.

FACE.   Sirrah –

SUBTLE.   I shall mar
   All that tailor has made, if you approach.

The chaos this admits onto the stage is incredibly bold for the opening of a play and suggests an affinity between Mamet and Jonson. The brokenness of utterance, set against the controlling underlying iambic pentameter, creates a seamless noise of argument; only Dol seems able to complete her lines, and then not exclusively, and every interpolation feels like it carries a gesture within it. But, as with Chekhov, what's most startling here is Jonson's commitment to the workings of thought under pressure, rather than exposition and clarity. The gloriously crude and ineffectual insults and threats that Face and Subtle throw at each other have a misfiring truth to them, indicative of a mind hurling out its contents pell-mell – 'I fart at thee' is fabulously inane as is the riposte about licking figs, which in this case means piles. Face's unconvincing threats, despite being backed up by a weapon, inspire in Subtle a wonderfully opaque, surreal utterance ('O, let the wild sheep loose').

This scene reveals three figures all at the same pitch of intensity and therefore sharing a common tempo of thought and utterance, which the turn-taking and brevity of the lines reflects. It's also a model three-hander in the sense that all the participants have their roles in language clearly defined and there is a kind of equilibrium that's machine-like about the workings of the scene – for who can have the last word in such an interchange?

Jonson's antagonists are in a common state of rage. A rather less hectic and more considered scene, pitting spontaneity against calculation, comes in Act Three of *Othello*. In what is in many respects the first truly psychologically focused play, Iago acts here as a malevolent counsellor, a depraved shrink experimenting on the hapless Othello. The effect of double-vision within the scene is caused by the two tempos of thought at work, as Iago contemplates and improvises, whilst Othello absorbs the implications proffered to him. It's a long sequence from which two contrasting moments can stand for the whole:

IAGO. My noble lord –

OTHELLO.   What didst thou say, Iago?

IAGO. Did Michael Cassio, when you woo'd my lady,
    Know of your love?

OTHELLO. He did, from first to last... why dost thou ask?

IAGO. But for satisfaction of my thought.
    No further harm.

OTHELLO.   Why of thy thought, Iago?

IAGO. I did not think he had been acquainted with her.

OTHELLO. O yes, and went between us very often.

IAGO. Indeed?

OTHELLO.   Indeed? Indeed: discern'st thou aught in that?
    Is he not honest?

IAGO.   Honest my lord?

OTHELLO. Honest? Ay, honest.

IAGO.   My lord, for aught I know.

OTHELLO. What dost thou think?

IAGO.   Think, my lord?

OTHELLO. Think, my lord? By heaven, he echoes me,
    As if there were some monster in his thought,
    Too hideous to be shown [...]

The convergence of idiom, the reiterated questions, the exquisite insinuation here, reveal the sudden opening up of doubt in Othello. The latter's innocuous offering of too much information in response to Iago's innocent query provides the aperture Iago needs, but again reveals the living quality of speech. However rehearsed this scenario might have been in Iago's thoughts, it would always in practice require opportunism and immediacy, and his questions function as a kind of vamping. The short line of Iago's 'Indeed' creates a wonderfully apposite pause, and we see Othello hooked (there's a momentum of departure in the opening of the exchange which seems to cease here; Iago's first question, tucked into the close of their interchange, is all the more insidious in its mimicry of an afterthought). Iago's seeming obtuseness concerning Cassio's 'honesty' after the specificity of his first conversational gambit deepens the sense of intrigue and guardedness; he is playing someone who is enacting an interval between thought and speech, something Othello is largely incapable of doing. Iago's tease of setting in motion a train of thought and then seeming to forestall on it creates vertiginous effects of inwardness.

What makes this scene so horrifying is that we see Othello's innocence ravaged in real time before us; it's one of the most extended duologues in Shakespeare, and anticipates the power and starkness of a play like *Oleanna* in its interplay of intimacy and violation. What's so striking in the language is the way it represents Othello doing the violence to himself and then retreating in the closing stages to an unreachable inwardness:

> IAGO. [...] I humbly do beseech you of your pardon,
>   For too much loving you.
> OTHELLO.   I am bound to thee for ever.
> IAGO. I see this hath a little dash'd your spirits.
> OTHELLO. Not a jot, not a jot.
> IAGO.   I'faith I fear it has.

Iago's emollience and seeming solicitousness is all the more disgusting given what he has achieved, but again the performance of humility and loyalty is horribly well done. What's doubly shocking is Iago's sadism as he prods Othello out of his pit of introspection, the wounded bravado of 'Not a jot, not a jot', with its childlike understatement, evidence of Othello's habitual grandiloquence now stunned into cliché. Again what makes this dialogue so numbingly real is its immediacy, the manner in which Iago feeds off the unfolding collapse of Othello, offering us a script of the inner life of the scene.

Perhaps the most sure-footed and innovative practitioner of dialogue in our time is Caryl Churchill. In the closing act of *Top Girls* she achieves the most terrifyingly raw argument in modern theatre. Velocity of thought into verbalisation is again key here, especially as we are in the presence of two sisters, estranged and unreconciled, who know each other too well and within whose presence even the slightest implication is amplified immediately into accusation. Marlene, the central character of the play, has been lured from her corporate London life to the rural kitchen of her sister Joyce, through the subterfuge of Angie, Marlene's unclaimed daughter, who many years before she placed in Joyce's charge. In this scene, Marlene's motor is running fast; she's arrived under false pretences at the place she fears and loathes most, and finds herself ill-prepared to sustain the persona of her new self under the steady, acute gaze of her sister, who has made that persona possible. But what is most striking in the writing is the way in which Churchill maps their crossing of the Rubicon, as their words wound to such an extent that no remission can follow.

MARLENE. I came up this morning and spent the day in Ipswich.

I went to see mother.

JOYCE. Did she recognise you?

MARLENE. Are you trying to be funny?

JOYCE. No, she does wander.

MARLENE. She wasn't wandering at all, she was very lucid thank you.

JOYCE. You were very lucky then.

MARLENE. Fucking awful life she's had.

JOYCE. Don't tell me.

MARLENE. Fucking waste.

JOYCE. Don't talk to me.

MARLENE. Why shouldn't I talk? Why shouldn't I talk to you? / Isn't she my mother too?

JOYCE. Look, you've left, you've gone away, / we can do without you.

MARLENE. I left home, so what, I left home. People do leave
    home / it is normal.

JOYCE. We understand that, we can do without you.

MARLENE. We weren't happy. Were you happy?

JOYCE. Don't come back.

MARLENE. So it's just your mother is it, your child, you
    never wanted me round, / you were jealous of me
    because I was the

JOYCE. Here we go.

MARLENE. little one and I was clever

What's breathtaking here is the way the argument is wilfully
entered into and then exceeds the participants' control. The
sudden shifts to confrontation force the characters to release
increasingly uncontrollable feelings rendered in overlaps,
incomplete sentences, petulant mutual accusation and, in Marlene's case, repellent self-pity. The opening is characteristic:
Marlene's gambit about their mother (always 'mum' for Joyce)
is clearly a provocation but also an appropriation; Joyce's
tellingly callous and disingenuous piece of realism is the *casus*
belli Marlene is waiting for – she's trying to draw Joyce's fire so
her thinly concealed desire for self-justification can be legit-
imised. The moment before the storm of full-on confrontation
is caught chillingly in Marlene's bid for hard-boiled feminist
insight ('Fucking awful life she's had'), which Joyce parries but
doesn't affirm. Marlene's flaunting of her urbane detachment
slips swiftly into unmediated belligerence, and with Joyce's
retreat into 'we', the ritual wounding can begin.

As with Chekhov, this white-hot exchange is meticulously
constructed in its rhythms to simulate the rapidity with which
thought betrays itself in speech, and feelings ambush intents.
Here Churchill achieves a calculated inelegance and asymmetry
in the language to suggest rehearsed and tired sentiments
emerging almost automatically – as Joyce notes, 'Here we go.'
The unanswered questions which provide their own answers,
Joyce's easy slogans, Marlene's vindictive sarcasm – all enable
the true indignity of an authentic argument to appear, as in
Jonson, with all the lameness of quickly skimmed thoughts

and the recklessness of ill-considered accusation. Churchill more than any other writer has narrowed the gap between thought and expression, and as a consequence the scene is hot with unresolved feeling. Her dialogue ensures the audience do not simply witness the heat of the scene, but are burned by it as surely as the characters.

Chapter Seven
Dynamic Symbols: The Art of Suggestion

Peter Brook suggests that the acid test of theatre is 'what remains'. Given that the stage is inherently ephemeral, all great plays stamp their mark on our memory in the form of iconic after-images. *Agamemnon* is contained in the red cloak laid down like a net to trap the returning hero; *Hamlet* by a man in a ruff with a skull; *Woyzeck* by a man bearing his dead wife into a lake; *Top Girls* by a girl sleepwalking in a moonlit kitchen. How these images come to exceed their narrative brief and become saturated in meaning is more elusive. After all, every passing moment in a play potentially yields an image or symbol; but were every moment to do so, a play would grind to a halt. How plays secrete apposite symbols at moments of pressure is what this chapter concerns itself with.

Theatre inhabits a much sparer visual or sensory field than other dramatic forms (excluding radio) through its sheer selectivity. This is largely because of the economy and constraint the stage imposes. Plays therefore work through *synecdoche*, offering parts that stand for wholes – a room for a house, a tree for a wood, a family for a nation. For every object or person or place specified onstage, we sense the presence of those not there; every onstage suggests an offstage and the limitations of the form place symbolic weight onto everything populating the stage. A playwright's symbolic sense is less about creating symbols and more about controlling them. A playwright's power to evoke more than what is shown, most explicitly in their stage directions, but also in their deeper suggestive powers, enables the play's dialogue and action to create resonance beyond function. This resonance might be amplified by the work of the designer and director, but it is rooted in the primary suggestive force of the drama itself.

The Realm of the Senses

Theatre is an object lesson in the manner the Italian educator Pestalozzi envisaged – it communicates ideas through sensory experience that works on the ear and the eye to reach the brain. The sources of the playwright's sense-repertoire might appear limited in comparison to a film, but these limits make what gets into the play all the more expressive. After all, nothing on the stage is simply itself. As Caryl Churchill's short play *This is a Chair* shows, a simple prop is loaded with meaning: a chair is a throne, a ducking stool and a restraining device all at once. The interaction of character with set or property or costume, the interaction of physical action with spoken word, the interaction of theatrical elements (sound, light) with all of the above as specified in the stage direction, enable an image to gather associations – associations that move such elements beyond the functional into the expressive.

Clearly, different types of play capitalise on this tendency towards metaphor and symbol, to a greater or lesser extent. Lorca's *Blood Wedding*, for instance, marries a spare aesthetic of pared-back dialogue and unspecified locales with an explicit dictation of the stage image. His spaces in the final act are given a kind of colour coding, as in the closing scene: 'White room. Two girls in blue, winding skein of red wool.' The action of the scene seems motivated by the image of red wool spilling across a white space: the lovers are captured in the heat of their elopement and killed. Also in the final act, Lorca introduces the Moon into the play: 'Enter the Moon – a young woodcutter with a white face. Intense blue light.' This necessitates a stylisation of costume, design and performance, reducing the actor's body to a hieroglyph in the manner called for by French director Antonin Artaud. These portents and the colouration of the action are mirrored in the heightened dialogue, full of proverbs and reiterated images of wells, horses and blood, accompanied by duende songs, serving to inflect each moment with archetypal import. Lorca's poetics offer a bold realisation of his contemporary Jean Cocteau's plea for 'poetry of the theatre' rather than 'poetry in the theatre'. He also reveals the two contradictory movements by which that suggestive poetic is achieved – through abstraction (removing particularising detail that limits and literalises) and prescription (the reiteration of verbal and visual images in counterpoint, the drawing on myth and song).

These techniques are emulated to very different effect in Sarah Kane's most suggestive play *Cleansed*, notably in the coloured yet abstract spaces: 'The White Room', 'The Red Room', 'The Round Room'. Here, resonance emerges through the tough juxtaposition of cruel yet non-naturalistic actions, with scenes often reduced to images and dialogue flattened into colourless simplicity. In fact, in the economy of the play, that richness of the visual and aural realm necessitates this demotion of language's role. This is evident in Scene Thirteen with its captive lovers, Carl and Rod. The scene begins with Rod musing over the savagery of the all-powerful Tinker. Then dialogue gives way to song and dance, as a child sings Lennon and McCartney's 'Things We Said Today':

> *The singing stops.*
> *Then begins again.*
> CARL *stands, wobbly.*
> *He begins to dance – a dance of love for* ROD.
> *The dance becomes frenzied, frantic, and* CARL *makes grunting noises, mingling with the child's singing.* [...]
> TINKER *is watching.*
> *He forces* CARL *to the ground and cuts off his feet.*

As in Lorca, the action is sensorily precise; what makes it suggestive is precisely the removal of words and therefore voiced intentions. It has an implacable quality, flouting rational explication. Likewise, the play offers an answering, visionary set of images which defy realisation, as in Scene Ten, when, after Grace has been horribly violated, 'Out of the ground grow daffodils. They burst upward, their yellow covering the entire stage.' Daffodils, not lilacs – suggestive of spring, renewal, indelibly romantic in association. There is, as is often the case with the theatre of symbolism, a nod to earlier traditions of sacred drama. In relinquishing dialogue for image, Kane both hands over power to the production (in the sense that Carl's dance could take a myriad of different forms) and at the same time constrains it (the *mise-en-scène* and action is meticulously mapped out).

There are dangers in this aesthetic. Behind Lorca and Kane's approach lies a philosophy of dramatic form made particularly explicit in the late nineteenth century and deriving from French poetry and literature. For poets such as Baudelaire or Mallarmé, and playwrights such as Wilde, the symbol was not merely a device, it was the imperative behind the work, serving to obscure overt meaning and reveal the world as a deceptive brocade concealing the spiritual truth. The epitome of this approach in playwriting terms is Wilde's *Salome*, a kind of total theatre where all the dramatic elements are choreographed to create a suggestive sensorium, and which also famously climaxes in a dance, that of the Seven Veils. Wilde's hopes for its London debut are revealed in his correspondence with artist Charles Ricketts: 'A violet sky and in place of an orchestra, braziers of perfume... a new perfume for every emotion.' Leaving aside this unrealised aspiration for olfactory effects, *Salome* as a play is pregnant with images of moons, blood and darkness; but in contrast to the stripped-back worlds of Lorca and Kane, Wilde's action proceeds funereally, as if the play existed only to give rise to the symbols within it. Through language and image, Wilde forges a sequence of *tableaux vivants* influenced by the visual arts, especially Gustave Moreau's paintings: Jokanaan (John the Baptist) in the cistern, Salome's dance, Salome kissing the severed head of the prophet, Salome being crushed by Herod's soldiers. *Salome* is an extraordinary play, and can work effectively onstage, as Steven Berkoff's astonishing 1990 production revealed; but, unlike in *Blood Wedding* or *Cleansed*, the balance between symbol and action, between specification and open-endedness, is awry – all power has been granted to the symbol at the expense of the life of the play.

Iconic Images

Such explicitly poetic plays put symbolism before everything else. However, all great plays generate moments that seem to exceed their function and become a summation of the wider action. And generally these moments occur at the ends of acts or of the play itself:

The Cherry Orchard – The servant Firs alone in the sheeted-up nursery.

Old Times – Deeley with his head in Kate's lap, Anna standing with her back to us.

Plenty – Susan Traherne as an idealistic young girl on a French hillside.

Edmond – Edmond caressed by an African-American man in a cell.

In these end images, the meaning of the preceding action is concentrated into a sort of diagram. The isolated Firs embodies what the occupants of Ranevskaya's household have lost and the fate of the world they derive from; the image also epitomises the lethal consequences of their vague, romanticised world view. Harold Pinter's image reworks the tableau that begins the play, of Deeley slumped on the sofa, Kate curled up on the chair, Anna standing looking in. The intervening action may have expelled Anna from their life, but it's also made explicit Kate's enigmatic power and Deeley's abject dependence. And Anna has not exited; the three remain, condemned to be with each other. The image of Susan in *Plenty*, given it is a retrospective one, enacts the enduring hold the past exerts on her bleak present and gives that past pre-eminence. As to Edmond, his quest has ended in a kind of thwarted romance, where he learns to love what he feared; the cell itself seems to embody his insight that 'Our life is a *school*house, and we're dead.'

Hamlet reveals how this process works throughout the play, as each act flashes up its own iconic image as a sort of landmark. Here is a selective account:

Such images suggest stasis, suspensions in the narrative movement – and they do all have a show-stopping quality. The Ghost after all walks in silence and is mute, and demands that we read him symbolically. Again, with the Player King, an image of stasis from an earlier tale, the moment before Pyrrhus slays Priam, is performed, apparently without immediate purpose within the scene. The Player King even has a startling break in the iambic pentameter to emphasise the stillness of this moment:

> So, as a painted tyrant, Pyrrhus stood,
> And like a neutral to his will and matter,
> Did nothing.
> But as we often see against some storm...

The image of Hamlet contemplating murder but not executing it, poised over Claudius's supplicant form, is rich in irony and consequently memorable. Likewise, Ophelia's excruciating performance to the spellbound Court, sliding in and out of song, and accompanied by the distribution of flowers and herbs, again arrests the action. Hamlet's happening upon the skull of Yorick in the graveyard, whilst hardly pertinent to the immediate narrative, has come to embody the meditative, morbid strangeness of the whole play.

Such images derive from earlier forms of theatre – the dumbshow (explicitly present in the performance in Act Three) and the tableau. They arise from moments that transcend the flow of narrative, assembling the inner meaning of the action into a picture that stands out in relief. This pictorial idea is dangerous – rather like a high-concept design, it might impose on the play portentous images that weigh down on the organic motion of the action. Yet the plays above are all subtly structured by these landmark moments that are more than the sum of their parts, and which gather the immanent meaning of the whole into something ambivalent and memorable.

Take the image of Firs, captive, at the end of *The Cherry Orchard*. We have been prepared for his presence throughout the act, with most of the household seeking him out so he can be taken to the station. In previous acts he has steadily been established as the family's link to the lost world of serfdom and the days when the estate was sustainable, as well as the shared childhoods of Ranevskaya and her brother. Placing a minor character at the close of the play might appear a sort of after-thought, as if he were forgotten luggage. Yet with all the invocations of 'new life' in Act Four, the residual presence of an elderly retainer in a seemingly deserted house (indeed in the 'room once known as the nursery') acquires a number of reso-nances. Gradually a piece of narrative information suggests a different level of meaning in the play.

Firs, as elusive in the previous moments as a lost pair of galoshes, acquires the status of an object; left behind when all the actors have departed, and speaking to himself but also the audience, he enters a moment out of the narrative as well as one arising from it, and becomes emblematic. The deserted Firs forms an image that reflects back on the play before, as well as out into the world beyond it, because of the values placed on him within the narrative and by the other characters. The image grows out of the action, belonging to it but also func-tioning metaphorically beyond it in the following ways:

Contrast – For much of the play Firs is seen only in the presence of groups and in the wake of his master Gaev; Firs on his own is unexpected.

Echo – The play begins with two people waiting in this room for the return of the family and ends with one left behind by them; these framing images, through resemblance and difference, acquire a denser degree of meaning.

Position – In the syntax of the play the last image is the lingering one; configurings at the ends of acts and plays function as a kind of after-image on the retina.

Inversion – The image is full of inner paradoxes; Firs is a
servant without a master, one who cares for others
abandoned by those he cares for, the representative of
continuity representing the end of continuity.

Whilst some images clearly initiate a play's action, others may
be its destination and final expression, for an image in effect
expresses an idea made concrete and out of time. Cleopatra
dead with an asp on her breast, Solness falling from his own
building, Faustus imploring time to cease – all are images made
inevitable by the inner moral and intellectual workings of the
narrative that preceded them, and which they cap and express.

Building a Symbol

The steady building and preparation of a symbol to prime it
with resonance beyond itself is part of the narrative work of
the play. Forcing the pace of symbols can make them appear
flimsy and forced; in the end the images that endure are organic
ones, which arise ineluctably from the story being told. This is
evident in the imagery in Robert Holman's plays, steadily fashioned out of the substance of closely observed reality. Take his
1988 play *Across Oka*, which concerns itself with relationships
between seemingly antithetical social systems (USSR and England), between generations (Matty and his grandparents,
Eileen and Jolyon), and between environments (Yorkshire and
Siberia). The play – which at points seems to disavow narrative
movement altogether for patiently mapped private grief – in
fact goes about quietly constructing its central organic image,
namely the fate of the eggs of a rare Siberian crane. The play
opens with Jolyon explaining how a Russian friend bequeathed
him two eggs he longs to take to Siberia, a desire frustrated by
his unhappy marriage with Eileen; and it concludes with his
grandson, Matty, on an expedition with the son of a Siberian
scientist to place the eggs in a crane's nest and thereby reverse
its imminent extinction.

The eggs are embedded in the narrative from the outset.
Nikolai, the son of the scientist, awaits their arrival with barely
concealed passion. He and Matty learn to tend and maintain

them under scientist Pavel's tutelage, and the level of care required is meticulously established, the eggs having to be turned, kept in an incubator, handled with intricate care. In advance of the story few audience members would ascribe value to the eggs, but the action incrementally endows them with heft and weight – they stand for the nervous bond between the boys, representative of two highly polarised cultures, for the tentative and lost thread of affinity in the past between the dead grandfather and his living descendants, and for the future of the confused Matty. Of course, as eggs in themselves they carry associations with birth, transformation and change. So when the final scene pares all other elements away to observe the boys deep in the reserve at Oka, their conflict expressed through the eggs, the tension generated by their fate becomes unbearable:

> MATTY *has the egg in his hand.*
> NIKOLAI. Matty, what else can I do?
> MATTY. Just shake my hand.
>> *A slight pause.*
>> NIKOLAI *shakes his head.*
> NIKOLAI. No, you are a very naughty boy.
>> MATTY *picks up the second Siberian crane egg from the incubator. He presses his fingers around them.*
> MATTY. I'll break them.
> NIKOLAI. No, Matty, you would not do that.
> MATTY. I would.
> NIKOLAI. Matty, you are a nice boy really.
>> MATTY *hits the two eggs together. The shells crack. The eggs break. The embryos come out into his hands.*
>> *Silence.*

Such tension would be inconceivable, were this to be the play's first scene. Holman, however, has carefully inducted us into the meaning of this act of vandalism and self-loathing. This moment then feels like the play's destination and its unmistakable power derives from the fact that whilst it feels unpremeditated it is in fact the inevitable working out of all the events that precede it.

Symbols Against Symbols

Frank McGuinness's *Observe the Sons of Ulster Marching Towards the Somme* is explicitly concerned with the malevolent power of symbols to fix and paralyse a culture into fatal inertia. Pyper, its protagonist, a veteran of the Somme where his fellow Ulstermen were slaughtered, opens the play by conjuring up his companions going over the top into battle:

> *Silence. As the light increases,* PYPER *sees the ghosts appear,* CRAIG, ROULSTON *and* CRAWFORD.

The dead have become fixed monuments in his memory – but the play dissects Pyper's misremembered past, which in its ossified form has condemned Ulster to decades of conflict. To achieve this revisionism, McGuinness confronts the baleful symbols that bedevil Northern Ireland. The red hand, an image of Ulster ascendancy, finds itself reiterated throughout the play, but the most striking account of the malign effect of symbols is evident in the extended scene, 'Pairing'. Here the play's four character duets all find themselves battling against one icon or another within the Ulster landscape: Craig and Pyper ponder a pagan remain on Lough Erne, Crawford and Roulston skirmish in a Protestant church, Moore and Millen attempt to cross a rope bridge, and McIlwaine and Anderson drag a Lambeg drum through a field. The stage is divided into symbolic spaces, a constellation of broken images suggestive of 'Ulster': religious, atavistic, ceremonial and physical. The burden of hauling the great Lambeg drum is particularly potent as McIlwaine kicks and beats it in frustrated rage, invoking an image of a nation flattened by its own mythology. The two men attempt to stage their own Orange March, but the symbol, wrenched out of context, is pitifully unsatisfying:

> MCILWAINE. [...] It's no good here on your own. No good without the speakers. No good without the bands, no good without the banners. Without the chaps. No good on your own. Why did we come here to be jeered at? Why did we come here, Anderson?
>
> ANDERSON. To beat a drum.

McGuinness's harrowing play reveals how stage images can detoxify and re-humanise symbols that have become deadly clichés. In effect he activates them as a principle of narrative itself: each section of the play is motivated by a thorough deconstruction of Ulster's myths embodied in icons – the blood sacrifice of the Somme itself, the battle of the Boyne which the men re-enact before going to their own death, the very land-scape of Northern Ireland, reduced as it is in the scene above to four poignant fragments that exacerbate the men's pain and confirm their fate.

Suggestive Strategies

A symbol's primary practical function is to intensify or con-dense the scattered and elusive meanings of the play. When in ordinary life we talk of something having 'symbolic value' we usually want to suggest it has a meaning beyond its price tag; in a sense we are suggesting it carries associative weight, mnemonic and 'sentimental' meaning. This same implication extends to symbolic things in plays.

Consider the ubiquity of symbols in late-nineteenth-century plays, many of which are signposted in the very title of the texts. *The Wild Duck*, *The Seagull* and *The Cherry Orchard* all fling the symbol into the audience's lap, and for contemporary audiences such overtness can feel crude. Yet as a tool of char-acterisation alone, these symbols earn their keep in the play. Chekhov's eponymous cherry orchard serves as a map against which his characters define and differentiate themselves, thereby condensing and expressing with great economy the wider meanings of the play:

LOPAKHIN   *Commercial opportunity*:
                 'If you break up the cherry orchard and
                 the land along by the river into building
                 lots, then rent them out for summer
                 cottages, you'll have an income of least
                 twenty-five thousand a year.'

RANEVSKAYA /GAEV	*Childhood and aesthetic meanings*: 'Oh, my dearest darling, wonderful cherry orchard! My life, my youth, my happiness, goodbye!'
FIRS	*Practical source of cherries for preserves*: 'Yes they'd send the dried cherries, cartloads of 'em, to Moscow and Kharkov...'
TROFIMOV /ANYA	*Evidence of waste and memory of serfdom*: 'And can't you see, looking out at you from every tree trunk in that orchard, every leaf, every trunk, those human beings?'

The unseen dimension of the orchard (like the attic room with its wounded wild duck in Ibsen's play) deepens its expressive powers. Chekhov refined his capacity to pull this off, from the often embarrassing crudeness with which the seagull is invoked and even at one point brandished. Ibsen, too, found more active ways of combining the symbolic realm with the physical, naturalist one.

There are a number of ways in which these transactions between the seen and the unseen might work:

Windows and doors

The space beyond the stage and how it is glimpsed is always critical to the potency of what's onstage, from the Nightwatchman hailing the offstage beacons indicating Agamemnon's homecoming, to Hamm peering gloomily out of the windows of the undesignated space of Beckett's *Endgame* at what appears to be a devastated wasteland. A window or door evokes the beyond, be it a hostile space, a space that can only be yearned for, a transcendent space or a constant threat. They are the most charged points of any set as they imply choices. The reason that Nora's slamming of the door resonates so profoundly in *A Doll's House* is because that door has been the very embodiment of the limits of her world. The door that keeps admitting radically different stories and realities in Caryl Churchill's brilliant short play *Heart's Desire* embodies this idea.

In farces from Feydeau to Terry Johnson, the door is the locus of anxiety and revelation – in a sense, all the action pivots on the relationship between the exterior door and the door to a cupboard or a garden.

Obscure objects of desire

Robert Holman's eggs have been noted, but all plays have their significant properties that make visible and felt the unseen elements of interpersonal relationships. These 'props' rarely bring inherent value with them but, like money, acquire it from their differing functions in the hands of different characters: Desdemona's handkerchief in *Othello* is a keepsake which bespeaks intimacy, but in its very insubstantiality reveals the fragility of reputation in the world of the play, all the more potent given the absence of other specified objects. Characters are often embodied in such objects – think of the ominous trace of General Gabler apparent in his guns, which defeminise his daughter Hedda and impugn Tesman's masculinity. Marlene's gift of a dress to Angie in *Top Girls* gets caught in a rip tide of symbolic meaning concerning clothing that stretches back within the play to Lady Nijo's language of gowns in Act One, and gives weight to Angie's apparent resolve to kill her mother; but it also makes Marlene present in her absence and reveals the ill fit between her world and Angie's as the dress estranges the girl from her context, making her look foolish and incongruous.

Resonant sound

Sound is perhaps the most potent of all forms of theatrical symbolism. Its immersive, associative workings conjure up acoustic images of the unseen in the audience's imagination. Some sound comes of course with its own semantic freight – cock crows suggest time, space and milieu, as does the intoning of Big Ben, or the whine of a police siren. Yet sound can play a more ambivalent role. One of the most telling sound effects specified in a contemporary play is the tinkle of a slot machine that accompanies Mark's sexual transaction with rent-boy Gary in Mark Ravenhill's *Shopping and Fucking* – on one level this unwarranted specific direction in a play otherwise notable for its lack of scenic specification is crude in its denotation: this is a world reduced to the cash nexus. Yet the poignancy of the sound, set against the ambiguous exchange we see onstage, makes it more haunting, less satiric in function. The notoriously open-ended sound effect of a broken string ('dying away, sad') that comes towards the end of Act Two of *The Cherry Orchard* is explained away by the characters as possibly the sound of a breaking mineshaft cable, or a heron's cry; but in itself it defies definition, largely because it has no clear narrative function.

Mise-en-scène

In a sense, this returns us to a kind of spatial thinking. When thinking about the set as a symbolic component in itself, the capacity of environments to bear their own allegorical, expressive power beyond story is apparent. Take Arthur Miller's *All My Sons*: here, the backyard of Joe Keller's house is less self-consciously located in the land of symbols than, say, Willy Loman's house in *Death of a Salesman*. Yet the picket fence, the porch and the evoked neighbourhood feel as if they have been drawn directly from an active Hollywood iconography that would have connected instantly with audiences of the day; that even now take us back to that eternal Capra-land that persists as an emblem of suburban USA (variously reworked by David Lynch and Sam Mendes). Thus Miller's garden works intertextually. But it is the broken tree, a kind of catalyst for the story but also a blatant portent, that tells us that 'something is wrong with this picture'. The iconic American house takes variant forms: the southern manse of Tennessee Williams definitively explored in *Cat on a Hot Tin Roof*, where it is slyly satirised by the vast bed that occupies it, a monument to the sterility of Brick and Maggie's relationship; the suburban house in August Wilson's *Fences*, which relocates Miller's domicile across the tracks to an underprivileged Afro-American world where even picket fences are not viable; the gothic pile in Tracy Letts' *August: Osage County*, freed of Williams's patriarch, rendering it a matriarchal remnant of hypocrisies and dormant rituals. All these houses function dramatically but also take part in a symbolic conversation within and beyond the theatre. The symbolic resonance of the *mise-en-scène* is confirmed by the fact that whole theatrical movements are designated by it, whether 'kitchen-sink realism' or the 'French window plays' despised by Kenneth Tynan.

Writing in light

Pace Brecht – who wanted his stage constantly ablaze in white light and thus rid of atmosphere – light before it gets anywhere near a lighting board is another eloquent part of the writer's symbolic repertoire. Beckett so often makes light function overtly as part of his stage language – even, as in *Play*, as a protagonist interrogating the figures in the urn. Largely, playwrights work with implicit light, arising from the temporal movements of the action. The real-time descent into night in the closing act of *Top Girls* is a classic example of this: there's no stage direction to indicate that Joyce's departure at the end of the act will plunge the kitchen into darkness, setting us up for the spooky re-entry of Angie, but it is implied in the scene, as is the movement from 'evening' indicated at the opening of the scene to night (e.g. Angie going to bed, Marlene reflecting on the fact that it's too late to go for a walk to the estuary). The long fade of the day is written in and helps symbolically nudge us and the sisters into a darker place of more irreversible confrontation. Ibsen invokes light's power in a masterly fashion: *The Wild Duck* moves from a lighting state depicting hospitality ('brilliantly lit lamps and candelabra'), to the single lamp of Ekdal's humble studio in Act Two, to the hopeful daylight streaming in from a skylight in the same room in Act Three, the sun setting in Act Four, and finally the 'cold, grey morning light' of Act Five – those lighting states carry the whole emotional journey of the play in sensuous, symbolic form. Conor McPherson's *Shining City*, too, in its transit of a day in a suburban counsellor's office, tracks the movement of light through the room to evoke its mercurial state, indicative of the disordered life of its inhabitant.

The offstage character

Godot is the extreme exemplar of this, and the huge weight of meaning attached to his absence is a testament to the potency of referring to but not representing someone onstage. The offstage character is invariably powerful – whether it's the invoked but unseen sales firms alluded to in *Glengarry Glen Ross*, the men banished from *Top Girls*, the unseen guests in *The Chairs*, figures such as Mac or the long-deceased Jessie who populate the imagination in *The Homecoming* – as to be absent yet always spoken of suggests a determining presence in the action earned without any effort. In the more profligate theatre of the Renaissance, perhaps this role is most clearly occupied by ghosts – Hamlet's father is ever present even if not shown, just as Banquo in his death is surely more potent than in life. After all, why are these characters not there? Because they are dead, in which case their legacy is still binding the characters in their absence; because they have withdrawn (think of Theseus in *A Midsummer Night's Dream* or the Count in *Miss Julie*), with the constant threat that they may return; because they exist inside the characters more than in actuality (the son in *Who's Afraid of Virginia Woolf?*, and *The Chairs*, the intended target in *The Dumb Waiter*).

This list merely itemises the many ways in which theatre creates meaning almost by default. Symbols, then, like theatre itself, serve to condense what is elusive, to make manifest what is elliptical, to suggest more than their literal meaning – they are a litmus test of the achievement of true dramatisation, for they reveal the play working through indirect rather than overt modes of expression. The more condensed the world and action of the play, the more it exists on the level of the symbol, functioning metaphorically – but if it is only located on the plane of the metaphoric, it risks breaking loose from the audience's reality altogether.

Chapter Eight
Forms of Feeling: Moving the Audience

There is a strange contract at work in writing for the theatre – the audience come to be 'moved' yet do not wish to be 'manipulated'. The task of the writer is to create stories that generate emotional responses; but if writers direct all of their ingenuity to that end, their work becomes ingratiating. Plays that aspire to be machines for laughter can be tiresome in their demand for the audience's approbation. Plays that endeavour to reduce us to tears tend to leave us cold and unyielding. The game of eliciting feeling, and allowing it to emerge without coercion, is the work partly of the actor and director, but primarily that of the playwright.

[157]

Furthermore, any play that seeks to arouse a specified, singular emotional effect is doomed. To seek to scare, repel, shock, enrage or arouse an audience for the entire duration of a play only yields crude work. What feelings does *Hamlet* evoke? Fear at the outset, but wonder too. Embarrassment perhaps at the obdurate refusal of Hamlet to endorse his uncle's Court. Alarm, even pained recognition, at the Prince's pitiful condition, expressed in his first soliloquy. Relief at the re-entry of Horatio, with an odd sense of hope at the promise of the Ghost. The complexity of feeling encountered within the first thirty minutes of the play does not abate. And in great playwriting, so precisely is the tale told that its inherent emotional meaning is never in question. The disgruntlement of Claudius must not and does not outweigh our pity for Hamlet; indeed, the day we find Hamlet contemptible, the moral meaning of the play will be lost for ever.

It is fascinating how rarely emotion is considered in discussions of playwriting, as if it were too vulgar a topic. Yet even as I write I am thinking of last night in the theatre, watching Alexi Kaye Campbell's play *Apologia* at the Bush Theatre in London, and remembering the withheld pain of its central character Kristin, a mother whose past political activism caused her to neglect her now adult sons. The play focuses on the sons' anger at their mother's recently published autobiography, from which they are once again conspicuous by their absence.

Kristin keeps us and her family at bay emotionally throughout the action – she's too sharp, too ironic, too clever to simply 'feel'; set against her irony, the reproaches of her sons feel naïve and self-indulgent. Yet at the end, when she is finally alone, there's a moment in the text captured magnificently in Paola Dionisotti's performance:

> *She begins to tremble, her body is taken over by a sweeping surge of emotion, something that has been restrained and repressed for many years.*

This image of naked pain, with its echoes of Mother Courage's muted scream, remains with me because of the tact of the writing, which withholds this emotional release until we've heard and seen what we need to comprehend it, and therefore feel it. As Peter Hall has noted, a child crying is sad, but a child attempting not to is far more so – the work of repression, irony and displaced feeling in *Apologia* makes the ultimate release of grief overwhelming in effect. I did, in fact, find myself in tears.

Yet this was not the result of the author shamelessly tugging at the heart. The division between intellect and feeling that often polarises our reflections on emotion in the theatre can be profoundly misinformed. To sympathise with Kristin we have to engage with her intellectually and psychologically; given her cool detachment it would be easy to feel rebuked and excluded by her, yet the weighting of the play's argument, embodied in a series of charged testimonies from her family and friends, pushes us towards both her culpability and her loss. In one of its finest scenes, her most 'damaged' son Simon, adrift in adult life largely thanks to neglect in the past, arrives at her house late at night, his hand bleeding – apparently from an accident en route – and sits at Kristin's moonlit kitchen table, whilst she picks glass from his palm. Yet even this eloquent maternal action is undermined by her infuriatingly reductive account of Simon's life, to which he can only respond in numb monosyllables:

> KRISTIN. I know you wanted to talk to me. And I want you
> to know that there is nothing you can't say.
>
> SIMON. Good.
>
> KRISTIN. However uncomfortable.
>
> *Pause.*
>
> I want us to be friends.
>
> SIMON. Yes.
>
> *Pause.*
>
> KRISTIN. Your brother is very worried about you. But I
> think he's got the wrong end of the stick.
>
> SIMON. Has he?
>
> *Pause. She is trying to tread carefully.*

The profound feeling conjured from these curt responses reveals again how emotion is made palpable through disarticulation – Simon's apparent complaisance in the dialogue suggests, in fact, reservoirs of controlled rage. The actor would discern this from Simon's monologue later in the scene, where he reveals a long-buried memory of maternal abandonment. Yet even without that speech, the writing subtly encodes our sense of Kristin's manipulative endeavour and her son's struggle to maintain control in the face of it.

How theatrical writing elicits feeling in the actor's body, which then alchemically conducts it into the audience's, is one of the great mysteries of theatre. The French philosopher Denis Diderot analysed it incisively in his essay on the 'Paradox of the Actor', who 'laughs when he cries and cries when he laughs'. Yet even more mysterious is the sedimentation of feeling between and within the lines of a play, like landmines secreted within an innocuous landscape. Below are some reflections on how such mines might be laid.

An Anatomy of Laughter

Laughter is the most fearsomely powerful indicator of a play's functioning. Actors crave it even in the most earnest of plays as some kind of endorsement of the performance. And laughter is not nor should be exclusively found within a comedy. To be deemed 'humourless' is especially damning on the Anglo-Saxon stage; yet it was Teutonic Brecht who commented that a theatre that cannot be laughed at *should* be laughed at. So how is laughter solicited from audiences?

The joke

Jokes or gags in plays are risky if they correspond to jokes in everyday life. After all, a joke is a self-contained story that could impede rather than advance the movement of the play; it might grant a local pay-off but is likely to form a blockage in the flow of the play's energy. The theatrical cannot afford isolated moments; a gag must be part of a pattern of jokes, building to a deeper sort of laughter. In that sense the joke is an idea, a revelation of character and an indicator of the world of the play.

Take the first act of *Top Girls*. We are soon given to understand the play as one that invites laughter despite its seriousness of theme, as Churchill's comic effects appear early in the evening. This is simply good craft: to open a play in the midst of tragic feeling is fatal, as we are not yet ready for it – the comedy of opening scenes warms us up. In the opening of *Top Girls*, the joke framing the whole act works through recognition and incongruity: the familiar scenario of a meal in a contemporary restaurant, set against the deeply unfamiliar ensemble of women partaking in it. This framing joke, embodied in the visual paradox of a miscellany of historical costumes set against that contemporary setting, is patiently established as the women enter and place their orders, with their choices of food and drink acquiring increasing comic potential. The recurrent monosyllabic interjections of Dull Gret, escapee from a violent Breughel painting, acquire particular cumulative power as they return after long silences (for example her order of 'Pig', then 'Potatoes'); the contrasting demureness of exasperating goody-goody Patient Griselda, a Chaucerian stereotype of docile femininity, with her anorexic preference for 'cheese and biscuits' over pudding, yields comic effects of recognition, as well as a local pay-off of the anachronistic scenario of the act as a whole – whilst cheese and biscuits separately might have been staple fare in the fourteenth century, the contemporary connotation as 'the slimmer's choice' is a conscious anachronism. Out of the scene's context there is nothing inherently funny or comic in any of this – the humour is specific to character and situation. In theatre all jokes are running jokes to the extent that, unlike jokes in everyday life, theatrical gags connect to the ongoing movement of the scene and work through repetition and variation.

Ironies

The philosopher Thomas Hobbes famously described laughter as a form of 'sudden glory', noting its link to the exercise of power. Power and laughter in the theatre are deeply connected, largely through the functioning of 'dramatic irony'. When the audience know more than the characters, this laughter of superiority can be harvested. In *Glengarry Glen Ross*, for instance, laughter is all about power; it doesn't take us long to realise that Moss is duping Aaronow and so we wincingly enjoy the way he catches his victim in a verbal web. Likewise in the dazzling second act we are made privy to Roma and Williamson's sting on an innocent punter and enjoy the wild, complicit laughter induced by their virtuoso improvisations at the expense of the uncomprehending client. Ben Jonson's *Volpone*, which also deploys the confidence trick – in this case Volpone's impersonation of a dying man with a juicy inheritance – is predicated on these sorts of bitter pleasures: in every scene we are made complicit with Mosca and Volpone's deceit, only to watch it play out in the presence of the duped 'gull', for whom Jonson, through archetypal comic characterisation, makes it impossible to feel any sympathy. But whilst in some respects the play licenses us to enjoy bullying, it undermines that with increasing discomfort as more ingenuous victims, such as Celia, enter into Volpone's trap. Jonson cannily pushes to the limits our tolerance of these fraudsters, just as Mamet laces our pleasures with the disturbing sense that we are all dupes like Lingk or Aaronow.

While one form of dramatic irony aligns us with some characters onstage against others, a more radical version makes us privy to some truths available to none of the characters. The misunderstanding, one of the engines of all stage humour, governs the entirety of Gogol's *The Government Inspector*, where provincial Russian townspeople mistake an unassuming traveller, Khlestakov, for their nemesis, the inspector from Petersburg. If Khlestakov had arrived in town with a deliberate intent to deceive its inhabitants as to his true identity, perpetrating the sort of fraud Jonson dramatises, the play would be far less giddying and generous in its comic impact. The fact that neither he nor his 'victims' are aware of the actual truth – something the audience is all too aware of – generates a wilder, more destabilising laughter. This anarchic hilarity also governs much of *A Midsummer Night's Dream*, where, at times, not even Puck or Oberon are ahead of the audience, and everyone is equally confounded in the comic conceit. The delirium of dramatic irony pushed to its limit is perhaps most evident in Joe Orton's *What the Butler Saw*, where nobody in the play escapes the ever-deepening misapprehensions within it, resulting in a nightmarish laughter, the plot serving as a Kafkaesque mechanism of comedy that far outstrips any character's control.

Recognition

For some people, the flurries of laughter that stir within an audience at the beginning of a play, when nothing obviously funny has happened, serve only to reveal the inherent affectedness of the form (rather like those knowing guffaws that greet a particularly obscure gag in Shakespeare). Yet there is something about this laughter that is intrinsic to the theatrical experience, and it concerns the workings of recognition, the audience's acknowledgement of the truthfulness of what is being represented. The opening of Pinter's short play *The Dumb Waiter*, where Gus and Ben do nothing very much for a very long time, draws waves of generous laughter from the audience precisely because the characters refuse to gratify any urge for action and heroism, and are so humble and idiosyncratic in their privacy. We laugh at our role as eavesdroppers on this unguarded behaviour, perhaps out of a nervous awareness of the impropriety of doing so. Likewise, after the interval the returning audience offers up gales of laughter in response to the most inconsequential of actions. This may well have something to do with the interval drink, but is also about our pleasure at meeting the characters again, recognising their quirks and traits, as if reconnecting with old friends. Equally, this laughter derives from the audience having some ownership of the story, taking pleasure in returning to a familiar world (cinema offers this only in the form of remakes, or television with a returning serial). It's comparable to the laughs and cheers that greet the re-entry of a character in a situation comedy (how will Kramer enter Jerry Seinfeld's apartment in this episode?). The laughter arising from the observation of truth is for me the most potent argument for the theatre – yes it can arise from glib generalities (observations about men by women, and vice versa; allusions to Scandinavian virtue or the mendacity of politicians), yet the correspondence between the depiction of a character or an action and the collective insight of the audience is one of the stage's chief pleasures. The laugh that greets such moments is equivalent to a shout of affirmation, to what Hamlet seeks in *The Mousetrap*: 'a hit, a palpable hit'.

Wit

Wit emerges from the capacity to make rapid and irresistible connections between apparently incongruous things – as Coleridge said when describing its effect in the work of the metaphysical poets, it offers 'heterogeneous ideas yoked together by violence'. For some, wit is a marker of smug urbanity and shallow cleverness; yet it appears in the most apparently hostile of contexts. Take Sarah Kane's plays, which, given their reputation for raw emotion, should perhaps be thought pretty inimical to wit. This is true if we understand wit in a narrow, verbal sense; yet in *Blasted*, the Soldier's observation after raping Ian – 'Can't get tragic about your arse' – still offers a horribly funny conjunction of ideas. Wit also flashes out of the despairing cantata of *Crave* at the oddest of moments: it is there in the form of paradoxes and moments of self-recognition such as C's detached description of herself:

C. She ceases to continue with the day-to-day farce of
getting through the next few hours in an attempt to
ward off the fact that she doesn't know how to get
through the next forty years.

Such sudden antitheses reveal the essential appeal of wit in moments of extremity – it heroically transforms pain into understanding.

The work of Kane's fellow 'in-yer-face' playwright, Mark Ravenhill, is also unashamedly saturated with wit, signalling his lineal descent from Wilde. Indeed, in Ravenhill's *Handbag*, wit is built into the very structure of the play, which offers a dialogue between the unexpressed queer subtexts of *The Importance of Being Earnest*, and rapid, slick images of contemporary gay parenting – a dialogue characterised by contrast, difference, affinity. This is particularly apparent in the brusque counterpoint between graphic sexual action and the mundane demands of parenthood; thus David, one of a middle-class quartet of gay parents, is constantly dragged away from his parental duties by the temptation of unprotected sex with his pick-up, Phil. The call of duty is manifest in one scene through the bleep of a pager as Phil gives David a blowjob; then, later:

> [PHIL] *carries on fucking* DAVID. DAVID's *mobile rings.*
>
> PHIL. You gonna get that?
>
> > *They continue fucking.*
> >
> > I think you better get it.
> >
> > DAVID *answers the mobile.*
> >
> > [...]
> >
> > PHIL *continues fucking* DAVID.
>
> DAVID. My kid's been born.

Here the wit lies in the rapid, contradictory dynamics of the scene: the hasty sex, the perfunctory call, the sheer indifference of David's hands-off parenting.

Rooted in cleverness, wit works through detachment. Ravenhill's scene is coldly erotic and comically mundane all at once, with David falling hilariously short of conventional expectations of a parent. It also confirms Coleridge's insight that wit works through juxtaposition. Sex and duty, conventional notions of biological parenting set against the contemporary possibility of distance parenting – these ideas and contrasts all adhere in this moment.

But such connections and contradictions need to be presented with great rapidity and economy. If wit is laboured, it dies. Take Anthony Neilson's *The Wonderful World of Dissocia*: as its protagonist Lisa enters the delusional world of the bipolar that is 'Dissocia', she is interrogated by an imaginary shrink named Victor, who, like all the figures she meets in the first half of the play, is as much a product of her illness as an independent person. Lisa has entered Dissocia by means of an hour gained in transit, as Victor 'explains':

> A seven-hour flight on BA from JFK with a two-hour delay on your UK ETA and a five-hour lag from EST to GMT just as BST is ending?!

Wit functions verbally here; the compression of information through acronyms, the jangle of apparently accidental rhymes, the sheer velocity of the exposition, parodically impenetrable like all bad exposition, transforms ideas and facts into pleasure and theatricality.

As a manifestation of the author's ingenuity, wit can pull focus from the characters and undermine the emotional impact of the play. Yet when, as in Neilson's play, wit is set against its opposite, embodied in the second half of the play by a drab psychiatric ward which makes us yearn for the colour and disorder of Dissocia, its absence is the clearest demonstration of its appeal.

Wit reveals the presence of ideas at work – judgements, observations, aphorisms – delivered at white heat. The reason we still quote Wilde is the density of his intellectual virtuosity, largely expressed through paradox and sly subversion. And wit can be addictive – the rapid turnover of ideas and connections in Orton's plays that entirely disarms the audience, making us surrender to a vision of the world we imagined we could resist. *What the Butler Saw* accumulates layer upon layer of absurdity and artifice, simply to articulate the unsayable in the midst of its mayhem. Thus in Act Two, the serial malpractice of lecherous psychiatrist Dr Prentice, under investigation by Dr Rance, leads to this absurd interrogation of the unfortunate secretary, Geraldine, forced by circumstances to dress up as a boy:

> DR RANCE. Do you think of yourself as a girl?
>
> GERALDINE. No.
>
> DR RANCE. Why not?
>
> GERALDINE. I'm a boy.
>
> DR RANCE (*kindly*). Do you have the evidence about you?
>
> GERALDINE (*her eyes flashing an appeal to* DR PRENTICE). I must be a boy. I like girls.
>
> > DR RANCE *stops and wrinkles his brow, puzzled.*
>
> DR RANCE (*aside, to* DR PRENTICE). I can't quite follow the reasoning there.
>
> DR PRENTICE. Many men imagine that a preference for women is, *ipso facto*, a proof of virility.
>
> DR RANCE (*nodding, sagely*). Someone really should write a book on these folk-myths.

Orton's overwhelming brilliance creates a seamless surface that conceals cunning insights into the audience's reality. Wit, here, is a weapon.

Fear and Loathing

Plays work through expectation. Screenwriter Frank Cottrell Boyce's observation about film holds equally good for a play: 'From the start of the film there should be something you're either longing to happen or dreading will happen.' The core emotional impact of dramatic storytelling lies in anticipation, which is why the opening of the play is critical and the ending so easy to fall short on. The game the playwright plays with the audience's expectations is central to the detonation of the play.

Willed frustration

The frustrated desire is the lynchpin of dramatic storytelling and is evidence perhaps of an inherently flirtatious aspect of playwriting. Taken too far, this is simply teasing – but crafty wrong-footing is essential to the dramatist's toolkit. In the first scene of Bond's *Lear*, the abortive drumhead trial, established to punish the worker accused of sabotage, threads its way through the scene like the whine of a dentist's drill. For the audience, the predicament of the Third Worker during the five digressive minutes following his summary death sentence is an agonising piece of unfinished business, exacerbated by Lear himself inadvertently blocking the firing squad whilst musing 'It's cruel to make him wait.' When the delayed execution finally comes, we've relinquished the hope of a pardon for the dull wish to get it over with.

David Mamet deploys this technique of deferral through-out his work, and nowhere more potently than in the exquisitely relentless *Edmond*. Edmond's desire to walk on the wild side in the city manifests itself in a series of deferred and digressive encounters – in Scene Nine, 'Upstairs at the Whore-house', Edmond's chance of receiving sexual gratification degenerates into a squabble with the 'whore' over money, far-cically concluding with him running out to cash a cheque. Mamet orchestrates this battery of frustrations and humilia-tions to egg Edmond on to the eruptions of violence which structure the play. Likewise, as with the deferred execution in *Lear*, Edmond's purchase of a knife in Scene Twelve, 'The Pawn-shop', seems to finally indicate his acceptance of the career of violence we have expected and dreaded hitherto. Yet whilst he considers the knife, the scene's end-line holds back: 'Let me think about it for a moment.' The action is not concluded and the scene ends on a suspended gesture, displacing its latent energy into the next scene. This suddenness of effect is reiter-ated in the opening of the next scene, 'The Subway', where Edmond stands beside a woman who is wearing a hat and with-out ceremony blurts out, 'My mother had a hat like that.' The previous scene is teasingly unacknowledged, but the elusive knife frighteningly resurfaces in the next three lines, when we might have assumed it altogether forgotten.

Such ratchet-like structures inform very different Mamet plays – *Oleanna* also enacts ninety minutes of willed frustration designed to turn liberal educator John into a benighted brute, kicking his student. The energy that charges Mamet's plays stems from the systematic repression of his characters – only when they're stripped bare of their carapace of civility can an almost religious calm establish itself (as in the final scene of *Edmond*, where Edmond and his cellmate acquire a zen-like acceptance that deliberately echoes *Hamlet*: 'There's a destiny that shapes our ends...').

Dread and the inexorable

Brecht considered tragedy reactionary because it implied the working-out of the inevitable in human life. In fact, inexorability is unavoidable in dramatic writing. The greatest heresy in any play is the contingent – the thing that happens without precedent, causality, any narrative logic at all. Artaud's short play *Le Jet de Sang* reveals how tiresome, even at ten minutes' length, an arbitrary, contingent theatre would be – characters change, the action swoops from image to image, tone jerks about, the whole thing is a contrived dream and therefore more pointless than a dream. In Brecht's own dramatic work, his theory is so often confounded. *Mother Courage* is a textbook example of condensing diffuse experience to create the steady drumbeat of the inexorable. The entire play is constructed around a hypothesis, namely that Courage's feeding off war will ultimately cost her her children. This thesis is concealed and revealed with consummate skill, rendered lucid through the play's images. The very cart that constitutes Courage's universe is stripped of its children with the rigour of a fable – and even if this is intended to signify the revealed workings of history rather than fate, it is experienced just as overwhelmingly.

This sense of the inexorable yields the primary emotional pay-off of tragedy – that 'ah' moment that Aristotle dubbed 'anagnorisis' or recognition, a term he used with reference to the protagonist but which has a wider application to what the audience as a whole feels. 'It cannot be – it must be' is the marginal note written in one of Beethoven's late quartets – it also describes the emotional insights that tragedy elicits. The art of controlling and conjuring up such feelings lies in rendering the inexorable action as irresistible. A magnificent example of this in practice is Marsha Norman's *'Night Mother*, where in real time a mother attempts to dissuade her daughter from committing suicide. The play's high-wire act is to place that terrible task before us in its opening minutes – the daughter announces her intention to kill herself and from then on the audience watches that objective approach like an iceberg spotted from the deck of the *Titanic*. But for the play to feel inexorable rather than wilful, the audience has to be satisfied that all the reasons for living must be rehearsed and exhausted; that we should have that terrible denouement set back by real hope, as the mother emerges from the sloth of her habitual self to become a magnificent persuader. It is undeniable that there is something perverse in such a blood sport, and in the wrong hands it can simply be piling on the agony. *Othello* is perhaps the perfect achievement of this effect, and for me it is unwatchable after a first viewing – there is an airless brilliance in its achievement of tragic dread, which makes the play unbearably close to the bear-baiting entertainments which in performance it might have been followed by.

Again it is necessary to go to Edward Bond's work for the greatest achievement of lucidity and inevitability – perversely because, as with Brecht, Bond passionately resists these very notions. The violence in *Saved* or *The Pope's Wedding* certainly possesses the lucidity of all tragic violence, yet Bond reconciles casualness and inevitability, his offbeat rhythms and sly accents refresh the horror he so potently rehearses. It's often forgotten that the stoning sequence in *Saved* is in fact not the climax of the play but its midpoint. If we need to offer causation for it, the play scatters clues as to why such an event is not just a grotesque piece of attitudinising, but arises out of the world we witness. The second scene, in which Pam wilfully ignores the wail of her child in favour of the charms of the *Radio Times*, prepares us for the drugged silence of the baby in the sixth scene, its doped state rendering it all the more prone to the torture inflicted on it. Yet the logic of scenic progression appears so surprising and casual (for instance, in the scene that follows the killing in which he has been complicit, Fred, the child's father, is abruptly revealed in prison on the eve of his trial, and his visitant Len notes with devastating understatement, 'They got the pram in court'), the dialogue is so unrhetorical, the writer's dramaturgy so stealthy and aloof, that we are utterly disarmed by the play's horror. Small wonder it generated such confused resistance on its first outing and still retains its power to shock.

So much of playwriting consists in preparing the audience for the emotions carried within the play. And a great deal of that process involves disarming the audience's inner critic, smuggling in detail under digressive fire to erupt later, planting things in their subconscious which then leap into the conscious life of the play. The opening of Caryl Churchill's *Far Away* offers an astonishing example of this art at work. As Harper tries to settle her niece Joan for the night, the ebb and flow of their dialogue steadily reveals what we dread through a drip-feed of expositional detail – an alarming world of ethnic cleansing emerges out of the rituals of a bedtime story. This dance of accusation, rebuttal and then counter-accusation between Harper and Joan is particularly powerful as one of the participants is a child – yet what's most illuminating about it is the way the ratchet mechanism works, with the twenty-minute scene structured around eight crucial questions and revelations:

Section one

> HARPER's *house. Night.*
>
> JOAN. I can't sleep
>
> HARPER. It's the strange bed.
>
> JOAN. No, I like different places.

The stark, suddenness of that opening establishes the rhythm of the scene; Joan's defiance and Harper's attempt to allay her fears:

> HARPER. It's always odd in a new place. When you've been here a week you'll look back at tonight and it won't seem the same at all.

Section two

> JOAN. I went out.
>
> HARPER. When? Just now?

Harper's intuition that there might be more to this than mere sleeplessness is confirmed; her previous line ('I'm going to bed myself') suggests an end to the debate, but Joan trumps her, deepening the risk by confessing, 'I went out the window', to which Harper tellingly replies, 'I'm not sure I like that.' A moment later it appears that this localised obstacle has been resolved ('Well that's enough adventures for one night'), but then the mystery deepens.

Section three

JOAN. I heard a noise.

The noise, which Harper explains away as an owl, becomes a 'person shrieking'. There is now no question of a quick submission to sleep; indeed it is apparent that Harper is now on edge:

HARPER. Now what did you imagine you saw in the dark?

Section four

JOAN. I saw my uncle... pushing someone into a shed.

The presence of the uncle transforms our perception of what's in store. This is no longer a tale of unmotivated fear, of a girl's apprehensions; there's now a more urgent mystery, compounded by an eerily precise act. Harper's improvisations become more desperate and fanciful, reminiscent of the improbable lies that spring from a character in a farce, inventing a 'party' to cover the uncle's anomalous act.

Section five

JOAN. There was a lorry.

Why is this lorry so troublesome? It indicates a scale of action that is systematic in its nature, and the ancillary revelation that Joan 'heard crying inside' panics Harper out of her apparent role as comforter into cautionary mode:

HARPER. There might be things that are not your business when you're a visitor in someone else's house.

Section six

JOAN. If it's a party, why was there so much blood?

The blood and the lorry take us into a place of real dread; Harper's disavowals now reach their absurd peak as she invents a dog called Flash to divert Joan away from the self-evident truth of the matter.

Section seven

JOAN. Why were the children in the shed?

This is the last sickening piece of the jigsaw; Harper will resist the force of revelation for one further speech.

Section eight

HARPER. You've found out something now.

The initiative now shifts entirely; while more details emerge, and Harper endeavours to lock Joan into complicity, effectively the scene is over, the cat is out of the bag and our imaginative construction of the offstage situation irrevocably formed.

Churchill subtly engineers this waltz of innocence and experience to permit a double movement of forward progression and retreat – Joan is too young and apparently powerless to come forth swiftly with the evidence of what she has seen; the gravity of what her aunt knows is literally unspeakable, and can only be teased out of her. The artfulness of the scene lives in the crafty laying of traps for the audience at ever-decreasing intervals. Each detail prepares us for the next one – at the point when Joan reveals that an iron bar has been used to beat children in a lorry, we're all too ready to accept it. Forcing the pace of that acceptance would risk the audience retreating into incredulity; here, Churchill's bland language and steady drumbeat of revelation neutralises the potential melodrama of the scenario. She staggers the arrival of each new fact to optimise its impact, devoting about two minutes to each fresh piece of information.

To get us to feel, the dramatist must compel us to believe. In *Far Away* our imaginations are worked over and made ready for an increasingly troubling evening. When audiences cry foul in terms of consistency ('she wouldn't do that') or probability ('that couldn't happen like that'), it is rarely the facts of the case that are in question, more the unfolding of those facts as something utterly irresistible. We don't question the blinding of Gloucester in *King Lear*, because the ninety minutes or so prior to that moment have mapped the disintegration of the moral values that might inhibit such barbarism; in *Saved* we succumb to the idea that a baby might be stoned to death, because we endure an hour's build-up to the act. Soliciting our belief takes time – film can trick us into acceptance faster only to betray us later; plays have to seduce us in something closer to real time.

Bloody good arguments

Playwriting is of course about conflict. Having bridled at that tired adage at the start of this book, I find myself endorsing it. But perhaps another way of saying it is that playwriting is dialectical, that so much of the power of any play derives from the power of argument within it. Simulating the emotive force of an argument is perhaps the acid test of any writerly competence. Since Sophocles brought his surgical stichomythic exchanges to the stage, finding ways of complicating that heartbeat of accelerating feeling and accumulating tension has been one of the key tasks of the playwright. For an argument must progress, it must be fired by a substantial rather than preconceived and rigged conflict. The playwright David Eldridge, a great crafter of arguments, has an exercise for dramatists where one character must stop another from leaving a room by using only a killer fact or revelation. The task of the playwright is to build up the fire and keep feeding its flames – because in real life arguments tend to stop in mid-flight with walk-outs, punch-ups or sheer inarticulacy, or become mere circular exchanges of accusation.

Oddly enough, it is a comedy that offers us the most dazzling example of quarrelling in dramatic form: Shakespeare's *A Midsummer Night's Dream* has, at its very core, the most satisfyingly achieved four-way argument in all of dramatic literature in Act Three, Scene Two. The electric confrontation is between Hermia (hitherto Lysander's beloved; now, thanks to the mistaken application of a magic potion to him, spurned by him), Helena (previously spurned, now adored), Lysander (previous adorer of Hermia, now of Helena), and finally,

Demetrius (prevous spurner of Helena and adorer of Hermia, now fixated on the former and indifferent to the latter). You sense the potential for confusion.

For comparison, the last incendiary act of *Top Girls* discussed in Chapter Six, where Marlene and Joyce finally have it out, helps further clarify the necessary conditions for the ultimate 'bloody good argument':

- **No exit**
  In the open space of the wood, the women perceive themselves to be vulnerable without men and therefore cannot part from their antagonists; the men, in turn, are besotted with Helena and thus won't leave her be. Most plays find a more defined setting that contains the argument and prevents it being broken off – for Marlene and Joyce, it's Joyce's home, where Marlene must remain since she is too drunk to drive and there's no other transport available in the middle of the countryside on a Sunday night; furthermore, given that this house contains the only family Marlene is prepared to acknowledge, leaving the situation, however reluctant she is to be in it, carries a massive cost.

- **No one is wrong**
  Michael Frayn, as we have seen, believes that in the perfect play everyone is right. Certainly, in the best arguments, everyone is right according to their own perception of the situation, and to that extent Hegel's account of tragedy being an expression of the conflict between two ethically correct contradictory positions has a bearing here. Helena has every reason to believe she is the subject of a grotesque prank; both men are ungovernably in love and, whilst their actions are ethically dubious, they are not in control of the love imposed upon them; Hermia has no explanation available for the shocking transformation of her friend and lover. Similarly, whilst Marlene is morally indebted to Joyce, her invocation of feminist principles to make sense of her decisions is surely valid.

- **The stakes are high**

  The best arguments in plays are between relatives or lovers because in such cases the participants are inextricably connected to each other. The most searing pain in the *Dream* argument is manifest in the breach between Hermia and Helena, who, Helena protests, in their childhood 'grew together, / Like to a double cherry... '; the reproachful reminder of their former sisterhood at the top of the scene brings home what it truly means for these women to be rivals. When those in the fray have a long, shared past, the potential for conflict is wonderfully enhanced. Marlene and Joyce move through years of shared experience and estrangement, and the argument is extended by their increasingly shrill audit of their entire lives.

- **Repressive effects**

  For a really alarming conflict, there need to be other pressures that seem to pull the participants away from the confrontation only to inflame them further. The contrast between the finely turned verse of Shakespeare's well-spoken brawlers and the increasingly ugly feelings beneath is essential to its impact; and, whilst it is a two-hander between the women, the secondary sparring and interventions of the men break up the relentlessness and serve to add further fuel to the pyre. In *Top Girls*, the repressive effect is Angie, who after all is the *casus belli*, but from whom the toxic secrets must be kept; Joyce and Marlene are initially kept on good terms by the comings and goings of Kit and Angie, but as the drink kicks in and the girls go to bed the true violence emerges.

- **Multifocal conflict**

  A great theatrical argument is embedded in layers of increasing gravity; moving from public to private, from localised to generalised, from past to present – it goes deeper because it moves through gateways into new situations of mutual knowledge and awareness. Helena and Hermia are amazed by the versions of each other,

the layers of desperation revealed by their spat, and a
sort of panic and delirium sets in until we reach a
ferocious exchange of insults ('Hang off, thou cat, thou
burr!' says Lysander to Hermia, implying a rough
physical repulsion; then she says to Helena, 'You
juggler! You canker-blossom!'). The improvised nature
of these affronts marks them out as authentic, just as
Marlene's vicious slanders of the working class and
Joyce's pitiful revenges on the 'cows' who employ her
reveal Churchill's unsentimental depiction of the
reductiveness of argument. Shakespeare can risk such
violence and irreversibility in his play because he is
conjuring up a universe where magic can bring humans
back from the brink of insoluble pain. Churchill has no
such recourse, so that when Marlene's 'But we're friends
anyway', receives Joyce's final, 'I don't think so, no', the
truly wounding nature of the argument is revealed.

For the audience in the theatre to feel emotion, we must either

share the emotion of the characters onstage, or, as in comedy,
experience an emotional counterpoint to the feelings of the
characters. We feel the emotions of Joyce or Marlene, Hermia
or Helena because we can understand them, we can, as they say,
'relate to them'. Allowing us to understand the feelings of others is a complex task: firstly those feelings need to be
articulated comprehensibly at a verbal level; but perhaps more
importantly they need to achieve sensory enactment within
the body of the scene – witnessing an argument involves us
enduring the stressful sounds of unresolved voices and raised
pitches which trigger our own physiological responses – as
Miranda puts it in *The Tempest*, we suffer with those we see suffer. Writing a bloody good argument is a way into the whole
craft of playwriting, to the extent that if we can believe the
argument, thrill to its meanders and reversals, experience the
high-pressure release of ideas within it and also be able to bear
it because the playwright has orchestrated its ebbs and flows,
then we perhaps can reach that state of *katharsis* so often
invoked in theatre but rarely experienced.

Act Three

Professional Secrets

Chapter Nine
A Taxonomy of Playwrights

Playwrights as an Endangered Species

Are playwrights strictly necessary or are they an anachronism, a species replaced by a cannier predator? If they do have a niche, should they come lower in the theatrical food-chain than their self-appointed place at the top?

Developments in the last century have sought to displace playwrights from their central position in the ecosystem of the stage. Much of this impetus has been out of a desire to release a kind of pure theatre – a total theatre liberated from the burden of literature and the word. And it is most powerfully, if not most clearly, articulated in the writings of Antonin Artaud in adages such as 'all writing is pigshit'. Artaud's febrile polemics, collected in a few terse volumes (expressed in the very medium he deplored), targeted the writer within the theatre. His attacks still draw blood.

Artaud was writing in Europe after the First World War, when the well-made play predominated, where the most outré theatre was rooted in naturalism and where, after the most devastating war in human history, the certainties of the conventional play seemed ill-suited to the realities beyond the theatre. But fundamental to his polemics are two ideas that need to be scrutinised. Firstly, that the text itself is inherently a kind of dead hand, subjecting the ephemeral logic of the theatre to something preordained and literary. The problem with a play is that it exists in advance of performance; for the crime of pre-emption alone the playwright stands accused of circumscribing the endless possibilities of theatre. Secondly, that the play is a thing of words, and words work at one remove from the body, and are inherently mediated; words bring a world beyond the theatre into the theatre, thereby violating its organic integrity. Language is inherently social and historical; the theatre need not be – indeed, it should be an escape from the social into something more immediate, communal and ritualised. If words are to be permitted into the theatre they can only function as matter for chanting and incantation; they must not point to anything beyond the moment.

On both counts plays must be found guilty as charged. The playwright by definition works in advance of the theatrical event, before any other theatrical collaborator is conceived of. The playwright works in the medium of language, even when shaping action or images through stage directions.

So Artaud's critique of writing cannot be entirely dismissed. But when you look closely at what might replace the playwright, the speciousness of his theories becomes more apparent. Indeed, those who succeed him and honour his tradition, if in more nuanced form, offer similar ideas. Two poles of endeavour are offered as a replacement for playwright and play. Firstly the notion of the *auteur*, collapsing writer into director, cutting out the middleman as it were, with the director writing directly with the actors' bodies, writing in light, costume, physicality, serving as what Artaud (himself a notoriously atrocious director who couldn't convey his intimations to even the most willing of performers) called 'the master of ceremonies'. At the other end of the spectrum, dispensing altogether with one governing voice, the joy of communality, the actors liberated from literature, merrily shaping their own vision, tuned in to their bodies, their sensibilities and the shared moment – free at last from being compelled to conform to the writer's prescriptive vision.

A close examination of the first tendency reveals that in the kind of theatre proposed to replace that of the playwright, plays are by no means absent from the picture – rather that writing becomes 'material' to suit the caprice of a director's vision. Tellingly, Artaud, in a footnote to one of his manifestos, proposes a season for his notional Theatre of Cruelty, and plays are on the agenda – *Woyzeck*, *'Tis Pity She's a Whore* (albeit shorn of dialogue). Then, during the brief lifespan of Artaud's Alfred Jarry Theatre, squeezed into the odd night in dark theatres in Paris, plays again featured, whether new works by his surrealist collaborator Roger Vitrac (*Victor*, *The Mysteries of Love*), or abused works by Paul Claudel, or straight versions of Strindberg's *A Dream Play*. Indeed the sole production that ensued from the publication of the manifestos, *The Cenci*, was a roughly dramaturged version of Shelley's verbose verse drama which, despite its scandalous subject matter, remained a play, albeit a turgid one. Plays – and other forms of literature – seemed to have some role in this liberated theatre; all that had changed was their status, now treated as artefacts to be eviscerated, vestiges of a tradition to be disavowed – but still essential to the theatre event.

Most of these new super-organisms proved less carnivorous than Artaud had threatened. Peter Brook, his great successor, has rarely dispensed with plays or indeed texts, whether turning to Ted Hughes to fashion a new language, collaborating with Jean-Claude Carrière or remaking Shakespeare. Likewise, contemporary directors such as Katie Mitchell, or even Emma Rice of Kneehigh, rarely abandon text altogether, even if it is dethroned and treated as a pretext for their own creation. Similarly, the devising tradition so often evolves into a rediscovery of writing by other means, the collective delegating the task to a single voice (Tim Etchells in the case of Forced Entertainment, Simon McBurney for Complicite). No one would deny the enormous excitement and integrity of this tradition of theatre-making, but its circumventions of writing often just lead to the ushering in of plays and playwrights under new terms.

Artaud felt that the words of the dramatist prevented the full gorgeous being of the theatre from being allowed to speak in its own voice. Yet his seductive vision of liberated theatricality – black light, warehouse spaces with the audience at the centre, chanting, screaming, quadrophonic sound – have congealed into a set of clichés that might enliven a school devising project, but in themselves are as hollow as the bombastic sound-and-light show at a heavy-metal gig. In the end, if theatre is to stir us deeply rather than simply turning up the volume, it needs the playwright to speak deep truths to us.

So what are the competencies that underpin the craft of playwriting? This book has so far focused on plays, but what knowledge and aptitudes do their creators possess?

There are barriers to an investigation into the nature of a playwright, thrown up by the way in which the history of theatre is usually perceived. Too often playwrights are divided up, corralled from each other in categories determined by era or form, and are thereby divided and ruled. The zoological gardens in which they are penned and maintained by academic propriety or critical platitude can obscure connections between them. Euripides has more in common with Joe Orton than he does with Aeschylus, while Sophocles has a bone to pick with Caryl Churchill. Trapped in the genre compound, the tragedians pace their cage, craving admission to the wild party that the comedians are throwing next door. Playwrights might seem categorisable by genre, nation and era, but playwriting is truly a transnational, hybrid endeavour. Maybe there's a way of thinking about playwriting that can reveal what's common to seemingly disparate writers in varying times and places? Just as a naturalist might identify a bird from its nest and flight or a mammal from its tracks, can we make out the playwright in the scattered traces they leave in the bodies of plays?

The Playwright as Outsider

Picture the first day of rehearsals. The actors slope in, reacquaint themselves with each other. The director works the room, armed with anecdotes. The stage manager gets the coffees in. The lighting designer sits impassively during the read-through, doodling and anticipating problems. The set designer tinkers with a model box and gossips about the show that's going tits-up down the road. And there, sitting in the corner with manuscript, thermos flask and pencil, is the playwright, seemingly entirely superfluous.

Like some visitant from another world, the playwright watches events unfold, revels in the thrill of their work that's now the property of a team of some thirty people, observes the actors' laser-like intelligences burning into their text, watches the director gently negotiate the actors' anxieties; but when the day's work is done, when the actors head off to the pub or to an audition, and the stage manager marks up the space, the director turns to the playwright – and the conversation that was always necessary, that was the reason for their being in the room, begins.

There but not there. Present yet absent. There are many playwrights who would reject this limited role, and very often they cross the boundary, become directors or get labelled difficult. Yet now at the end of the read-through, the actors seek out the writer in corners or in intervals and the questioning begins. There is a reality in any play, and the writer is its final arbiter. Worried queries emerge about the playwright's research, the genesis of the play, a scene, a line – and suddenly the author becomes indispensable. And then four weeks later, after the nightmare of the technical rehearsal where the play has been anatomised into hundreds of tedious bits, as it finds its final form, the playwright is again indispensable, called in to answer those perennial questions: 'Is this right? Is this what you meant?'

Debates about ownership of text in the theatre have raged since the Renaissance; but when things go wrong, when the critics tear into the social fabric of the play, the person indicted is the playwright, the bringer of the story.

This is as it should be. David Mamet was once asked if play-writing was a collaborative endeavour – his facial expression revealed a contempt memorable for its clarity. Yes, actors might work on his plays, he might work with others, but in the end play-making is the job of the playwright alone. Mamet represents an extreme and rather bracing pole of the debate – but implicit in the notion of compulsory collaboration, there is a risk of a drift to the lazily consensual. For there is a hierarchy of creation; without the play the actor cannot act, the director cannot direct, the designer cannot shape what Peter Brook calls

the 'virtual geometry' of the play. And whilst a foolish writer fails to amend and enliven their text in rehearsal or in dialogue with their collaborators, this comes after the essential process of private creation that brings all these artists together.

For some this is simply too undemocratic. But perhaps, as the great English critic William Hazlitt said, art *is* undemocratic. Since Michel Foucault asked 'What is an author?', dismembering the concept even as he became the most cited author of his day, or since Roland Barthes pronounced the death of the author in order to empower the reader, the isolated author has been deemed anachronistic. Individual authorship in some theatrical circles has been imagined as inherently fascist, patriarchal, phallocentric, phallogocentric – only collective creation is able to overcome such thought-crimes.

But the singularity of the playwright derives from their role as insider and outsider, a kind of Janus, in the fo'c's'le of theatre, looking ahead and behind. Theatre is, yes, collaborative, but collaborative only at specific moments. The playwright does not jump up on stage and shove aside the actors during the show. The playwright does not (or should not) bark notes at the actors in performance, or have a bash at knocking up their own design, or go on cans to cue the actors. Some individual playwrights may do all of these things – but the role of playwright does not demand them nor benefit from them.

Each collaboration happens in its own sphere, with its own logic at its own point. Of course there is a spectrum here from the painfully shy playwright who sits in a rictus of pain as the actors rehearse and goes home to curse them, to the 'man of the theatre' gaily tossing off rewrites, hobnobbing with actors and penning roles for Judi Dench. Yet like all divisions of labour and function (executive from legislative, private from public, doctor from patient), there is a logic and virtue in the separation of the role of the writer from that of the theatre-maker. And key to that separation is the playwright's role as iconoclast.

The Playwright as Iconoclast

Heiner Müller claimed he wrote his iconoclastic play *Hamlet-machine* to destroy Shakespeare. Harold Pinter has talked of the first night of *The Homecoming* in New York and his desire to assault the audience. Joe Orton mused on The Living Theatre's success in that same city through staging raw sexual contact with the audience and concluded that only sex would really 'fuck them up' – by which he meant the bourgeois theatregoers. Peter Handke set out to offend the audience. Sarah Kane's uncompromising *Blasted* intentionally broke apart the theatre consensus of the time, inducing fainting fits and walkouts in the process. As Peter Brook once defiantly proclaimed apropos audience derelictions from his production of John Arden's *Serjeant Musgrave's Dance*, 'Oh, for empty seats.'

Okay, that last statement of intent is from a director. But the path-breaking moments in theatrical evolution have arisen from playwrights writing plays that initially made no sense to producers or audience, shocking the stage into ever new forms. In the infancy of the theatre, playwrights and stage appeared to advance in lockstep – but even in fifth-century Athens, Euripides' *The Trojan Women* or Aristophanes' *Lysistrata* pushed the limits of what the audience could accept. In the Renaissance, Marlowe and Shakespeare pushed the play form as hard as they could towards the modernity they discerned in the audience, straining against the limits of patronage and censorship. The notion of the avant-garde proper, where writers conceive themselves as being truly in advance of their audience, is often deemed to have emerged in the nineteenth century with the Romantics. It could also, in theatrical terms, be pinned to Henry Fielding bringing down the full force of the law on his own head for coruscating satires such as *The Historical Register of 1736*, a play that repudiated the safe, licensed stage of his day and for which he had to devise his own theatre with its own rules and norms. This play, in a revue format that anticipates the political theatre of the twentieth century, its thinly veiled portraits of living politicians and its metatheatrical form, fusing satire on theatre with assaults on corruption, was so radical that the first Prime Minister, Robert Walpole, devised an Act of Parliament to silence the author. This statute constrained the English stage until the advent of Edward Bond.

This pattern – of playwrights breaking apart received forms and ideas, of plays written to refute the stage values of the day at the same time as repudiating the values of their times – continued, intermittently, through the next three hundred and fifty years. Goethe and Schiller articulated a new national identity in fractured Germany and in so doing broke with the tired classicism of the decorous French stage; their writing inaugurated a revolution in theatrical practice that presaged the political and social revolutions to come. Büchner's *Woyzeck*, though it took eighty years to reach the stage, foreshadowed both Naturalism and Expressionism in its form – and this from a playwright who never saw his work staged. Ibsen's plays were more widely experienced in publication than in performance and sent shock waves of cultural change through Europe, throwing up the innovations in acting and production that emerged under directors André Antoine in France or Konstantin Stanislavsky in Russia. The latter devised a whole theory of acting primarily in order to make sense of the initially tonally incomprehensible plays of Chekhov, redeeming *The Seagull*, which was greeted with utter bafflement in its first production. Then Alfred Jarry in his surrealist *Ubu Roi* rent the frail fabric of realism, inaugurating a new aesthetic that mirrored the collapse of humanist values across Europe and paved the way for Artaud's experiments.

All these breaks in habit, assaults on custom, infringements of public order, violations of taste, are acts of authorship. It is impossible to imagine the theatre in itself achieving such shifts because the theatre is an institution, collaborative, consensual and so on – and only the wayward, wilful, childish, intemperate and private work of the playwright is free enough to shake it and its audiences to their foundations.

'Creative destruction' is a familiar paradox. Inherent in every moment of playwriting is the desire to demolish, to clear a space, to open up a moment, to refuse. This is perhaps true of all writing, but it is magnified in theatrical writing because of the public nature of the endeavour. The poet and novelist speak to other private souls; the playwright envisages between their manuscript and its realisation a phalanx of other people: their peer writers, the writers that preceded them, the ever-expanding repertoire, literary managers, artistic directors, sceptical actors, hostile critics – and then the audience itself, so easily characterised as the enemy, so often deemed bourgeois, cast in the role of the society they resist in their bones. Is aggression so central to any other art form? Playwrights live in constant fear that what they do is an act of folly; surely they should seek to please that parade of people, ingratiate themselves with all their potential audiences? Yet in doing so, how quickly the public's contempt ensues.

The fighter doesn't always just square up to the opposition and land a blow. As some martial arts show us, retreat may be the best form of attack. Brecht provides a fabulous toolkit of stealth tactics, wintering out National Socialism by creating his own counter-court; playing the long game and landing in Berlin in 1947, equipped to build the theatre he'd planned during ten years of exile. Adriano Shaplin, Anthony Neilson and Howard Barker build their own counter-stages, redefine the rules to accommodate their own unruly talents. Playwriting is a fight for space, for attention, even for oxygen, and like all campaigns sometimes it is about laying siege, sometimes about retreating to gather strength. But in the ecosystem of theatre, the catalytic role of the playwright, rooted in their apartness from theatre-making, is essential to prevent theatre simply becoming about itself, content with artifice and familiar pleasures.

The Playwright as Sociologist

Sociology has got itself a bad name. We think of men with sideburns and leather-patched jackets on Open University broadcasts. We think of incomprehensible French social thinkers muttering about '*idéologie*'. We think brown. We think seventies. Yet one of the defining qualities of a strand of playwrights is their capacity to bring to the stage worlds alien to the audience – or, if known, so familiar that they need defamiliarising. In order to forge such worlds, the playwright must have antennae for the detail of how life is lived.

Writers draw on their own worlds, known realities that they bring to the stage. Take Arnold Wesker. Before *Chicken Soup with Barley* or *I'm Talking About Jerusalem*, there was no authoritative representation of the leftist Jewish East End community, which he revealed to his audience as the true storytellers of their time. Wesker's achievement ushered in the great wave of realism that washed onto the stage in the fifties and sixties, bringing unknown worlds to the theatre: David Storey's Yorkshire, Shelagh Delaney's Lancashire, David Rudkin's Worcestershire, Peter Gill's Cardiff. These writers instilled in the theatre of their day a new respect for different forms of work, a new delicacy in rendering domestic worlds, to expose injustice but also to document how we live. The shock of their work was less the presence of this sociological quality, and more the nature of the worlds being dramatised. The preceding generation of writers, such as Rattigan, Coward or Ackland, carried out comparable dissections of the worlds of Bohemia or lower-middle-class suburbia. The impulse to show the ways of the world is always present in theatre, from the representation of foreigners like Thebans and Trojans in tragedy, to Mystery plays that celebrate the practices of the medieval guilds that staged them (such as the so-called York Realist's account of the Crucifixion that was performed by a guild of nail-makers and was thus attentive to the mechanics of nailing Christ to his cross). Then there are the citizen comedies of Dekker or Jonson, which look closely at the world of trade through its vernacular. Restoration comedies, such as Farquhar's *The Recruiting Officer* or Goldsmith's *She Stoops to Conquer*, make comic capital out of the rituals and habits of provincial England.

The sociological cast of playwriting long precedes the invention of the discipline of sociology itself in the nineteenth century, a development which only served to make more precise the radical naturalistic observations of Zola and Ibsen, who chose to turn the focus on the world of the audience and the middle class it often derived from. It still thrives today in plays such as Roy Williams's, documenting and critiquing the conditions of Afro-Carribbean life in the UK, or August Wilson's Century Cycle project, dramatising the experience of Afro-Americans in Pittsburgh. English stages have been enriched by David Eldridge hymning the uncelebrated working-class worlds of Romford, Nell Leyshon's elegies for the rural backwaters of Somerset, Richard Cameron's anatomies of Doncaster, Richard Bean's of Hull, Andrea Dunbar's Bradford, Ayub Khan-Din's Salford. The patient rendering of defined communities, with their shibboleths and taboos and ceremonies, is a strand of theatre that takes increasingly scrupulous forms – and with each new world comes a new revitalising language for the stage, a new patois or sociolect or idiom.

Shakespeare is one of the greatest sociologists of all in this respect. He creates worlds effortlessly: the cold, hard, protocol-dominated Roman world, quite at odds with the teeming, polarised images of history he renders elsewhere, where Justice Shallow, Falstaff and Hotspur bring their own contradictions into play to figure England forth. The history plays are rich in local reference, informed by Shakespeare's switching between rural Warwickshire and the mayhem of Tudor London. The internal consistency of these mapped worlds, which fuse direct observation with historical imagining – fashioning a fictional Venice from an observed Eastcheap or Rome from the Inns of Court – reveals again the playwright as social engineer and documenter. Even a play as apparently fantastical as *A Midsummer Night's Dream* lays out each of its worlds with care – an Athens of aristocratic mores and patriarchal propriety, marked by the laughter of the elite; the mechanicals' milieu, more porous, governed by guild hierarchies but essentially egalitarian and fraternal; the woods, dominated by inversion, the erotic, even the sadistic. Each world is fitted out with its idiom, its code, its dynamic, rooted in the varieties of human experience Shakespeare observed.

Sociologists do not necessarily belong to the world they document; when social scientist Michael Young studied and wrote about the lives of East End boys in the 1950s, he was evidently not part of their universe. This is often equally true of dramatists, but their passport into their chosen world is through a minutely grasped sense of language, their access to what Raymond Williams once called 'a structure of feeling'. The film director Ken Loach has claimed that it's impossible for an actor to 'play class' – that is, to simulate a class identity not their own. Certainly, when a playwright brings a new world to the stage, we are entitled to interrogate their authenticity in relation to it. Yet it is possible for the writer to attach themselves so passionately to a particular reality and idiom that they can make it their own, in the manner of J.M. Synge: a man of genteel Anglo-Irish stock, who lived amongst the peasants of the Aran Islands, saturating himself in their dialect, and claiming it for his own.

Plays stage behaviour. They reveal rooms, and show which people enter them; they reveal the stuff that furnishes rooms and the relationship of their owners to that stuff. They show how things are done, how processes occur; as Walter Benjamin noted of Brecht's work, they 'uncover conditions'. They are anthropological too, documenting family life and rituals, showing the pressures and meanings of work, the rhythms of interaction.

It could be argued that this type of playwright is an endangered species; after all, in the contemporary world the very notion of settled, identifiable communities, with shared values, practices and idioms, finds itself under increasing assault by pressures of globalisation. The long, slow reveal of Irish plays such as Brian Friel's or Conor McPherson's, which have added so much bulk and weight to the skittish modern stage, could themselves be mementos of those realities they sought to render.

The Playwright as Journalist

The playwright as sociologist is frequently suspicious of the playwright as journalist. After all, the former often has one field of concern, one territory that they map tirelessly and painstakingly. The latter, like any journalist, moves restlessly between terrains, considering none essentially their own. But equally the notion of playwright as journalist is rooted in the inherently topical nature of the stage; plays at their best are always events, and all dramatists have a radar alerting them to the immediate concerns of their audience, if only to refute them. To this extent all plays are species of punditry, ripostes, gestures against an uncomprehending or ignorant world; they are also incitements and provocations. The journalist might write more immediately for the next day, but the playwright too is inextricably linked to their moment.

The journalist playwright has a commitment to reality, but it is a commitment based on research. Equally, like a journalist, this species of playwright is primed to excavate the contemporary, has a taste for the topical and a forensic sensibility. At its most extreme their writing may shade into journalism itself; it's no accident that two of the key proponents of the 'verbatim' genre of theatre, Richard Norton-Taylor and Victoria Brittain, are both journalists themselves, and Max Stafford-Clark, the foremost director of this type of work, has frequently collaborated with journalists through his theatre companies Joint Stock and Out of Joint.

David Hare, David Edgar (a former journalist) and Howard Brenton formed a phalanx of playwright–journalists who forged a socially responsive theatre that mirrored the rise of the new journalism in the 1970s, seeking to, as Hare put it, 'ventilate democracy'. For some, such as Dominic Dromgoole, the promiscuous topicality of their work, its 'aboutness', relegates it to a secondary sphere of playwriting. Yet, at its heart, it is an acknowledgement of the public nature of the stage – and indeed theatre's role as a participant in contemporary life.

Oddly enough, the work of these writers is at its weakest when it most closely resembles contemporary journalism, where punditry too often trumps reportage. For dramatists, the key model is the dispassionate work of journalists such as Jeremy Seabrook or Nick Davies, which finds its counterpart in fine verbatim work such as Hare's *The Permanent Way* or his trilogy of plays about British institutions (especially *Racing Demon*), Edgar's *The Prisoner's Dilemma* or *Continental Divide* – here, topicality and sociology rub shoulders, and the vigour of an unfamiliar world finds itself shockingly well caught. To this extent, playwrights perform the task of 'muckraker' and their work is analogous to the novels of Upton Sinclair, exposing the horrors of the meat-packing industry in Chicago in *The Jungle*, or the backstage documentaries of film-makers like Fred Wiseman, giving us insights into contemporary institutions. Hare shows us how the judiciary works, how political parties emasculate themselves, how the Church stifles dissent, how privatised railways incubated disaster; Edgar lets us eavesdrop on intense diplomacy, or the shaping of Democrat and Republican politics in the USA. We leave their plays less with specific memories of characters and more with a sense of the workings of hidden worlds.

Most essential of all is the sensitivity of the playwright to the stories that need to be told right now. As I write, audiences in London are rushing to catch Lucy Prebble's play *ENRON*, which documents the collapse of the eponymous rogue firm under the tenure of its CEO Jeffrey Skilling. When details of the project first emerged, a year before the financial meltdown of 2008, for some it appeared an anachronistic endeavour: why dramatise the corruption of the late nineties when the company was now history, the political regime it thrived under swept away, the world moved on? Yet *ENRON*'s appeal and success confirms again how theatre is concerned with what Ezra Pound called 'news that stays news'. After all, the inner journalist within the playwright might illuminate the present by means of the past. Brecht was drawn to the horrors of the Thirty Years War in *Mother Courage* as the Second World War broke out, just as he reconceived Galileo in *The Life of Galileo* as Oppenheimer unleashed the atom bomb on the world. Shakespeare's *Richard II* was famously staged by his patron the Earl of Essex as a curtain-raiser for a coup; *King Lear* and *Macbeth* crystallise the anxieties of an audience moving from the settled reign of Elizabeth into the uncharted waters of the Jacobean Court. That lurch to the past is often driven by censorship or social tact – but the playwright as journalist is attentive to the anxieties of the day.

Playwrights look towards their own time because the stage feeds off a contemporary audience who seek novelty and instruction; yet like Walter Benjamin's 'Angel of History', described memorably in his 'Theses on the Philosophy of History', playwrights peer back at the wreckage of the past, seeing the present growing out of its aftershocks. Hare has recently protested that journalism seeks to remove mystery from the world, whilst art rediscovers it. This perhaps distinguishes the playwright as journalist from journalism as such – but inherent in this species of playwright, perhaps more than in any other literary medium, is a passion for the present moment and the conviction that theatre is a public event as vital as a political meeting or a trial. From *The Trojan Women* to *Talking to Terrorists*, the playwright as journalist seeks to respond to the question 'Why do I need to see this play tonight?'

The Playwright as Architect

It's no accident that when Ibsen in *The Master Builder* or David Greig in *The Architect* or Howard Barker in *The Castle* wished to dramatise the ethical dilemmas of the playwright, they used architects for their surrogates. The function of the playwright is not dissimilar to that of the architect, an idea promulgated by the late Anthony Minghella. Both architects and playwrights produce blueprints for a work that they will need others to realise and that will be achieved through a myriad of compromises and acts of persuasion; both rely on powerful social institutions to bring their private visions into existence; both produce a form of public art, even though the architect strives for permanence and the playwright's work is by definition ephemeral. Solness in Ibsen's play famously laments that he began by erecting spires and 'castles in the air' and ends up a realist drudge 'building houses for people to live in'; through this dichotomy, Ibsen presents his own trajectory from verse dramatist to naturalist; the notion of 'homes for people to live in' offers a useful image of the playtext as an embryonic event, an outline for performance that awaits those who will finally realise and inhabit it.

Yet there is a more fundamental affinity between these two activities, which might also be found in the work of the composer – a concern with structure and form. A play, like a building, is made out of disarticulated elements; like a building it needs to be robust, it needs to have carrying capacity and it needs to work; like a building, it will be put to uses by its inhabitants, namely artists and audiences, that it can't conceive of precisely in advance. Yet where the structures of a building need to unfold in space, a play needs to unfold in time and space.

All playwrights are fabulators and fashioners, and their key raw material is story. The discussion of a play's deep structures above confirms this. As with architecture, form must follow function. But for some playwrights, form is the decisive factor in choosing to tell one story rather than another. Think of Pinter's *Betrayal* – would we be interested in this bloodless triad of bourgeois adulterers were it not for the cool architecture of Pinter's reverse chronology, which locks them into their confusions like flies in amber? Likewise Pinter's model, Beckett's *Play*, which seems even more concerned to bury its boulevard theme in the dynamics of image and structure; so much so that once the triangulated tale is told, Beckett demands that it is repeated.

Architecture is about the disposition and repetition of elements in space, memorably described as 'frozen music' by Goethe; certainly, the implicit rhythm of columns and peristyles and keystones finds its counterpart in playwriting's reiterations of motif, event, set-up and pay-off. Master builders in theatre delight in the formal aspect of the art – think of architectural masters such as Michael Frayn and Alan Ayckbourn, whose work is so predicated on the pleasures of form. Neither is forbidding at first glance, perhaps because their tenor and social contents are often so familiar, and oddly, in Ayckbourn's case, impervious to social change (he has noted that in a revival of *Relative Values* the only change he had to make to the text was to update the price of a bottle of whisky). Yet it's no accident that one of France's most avant-garde film directors, Alain Resnais, has been drawn to Ayckbourn's work on a number of occasions; within his limited social palette, the playwright works an astonishing set of variations on the art of storytelling. Think of *The Norman Conquests*, his artful layer cake of three versions of the same weekend, where the whole is most definitely more than the sum of the parts – the formal ambition would not shame Norman Foster.

The fabulous construction of Ayckbourn's plays is often an end in itself, and in that sense he's a formalist, who enjoys symmetries, ironies, reversals and echoes for their own sake, beyond any specific social meaning. For Frayn, form is profoundly expressive of the core idea motivating each play; for instance, in *Copenhagen* those involutions and overlaps are expressions of the quantum physics that animates the foreground action of the play. The play examines the encounter in 1941 between Danish atomic physicist Niels Bohr and his protégé Werner Heisenberg, witnessed by Bohr's wife Margrethe. Given that this event is undocumented and can only be represented through an act of speculation, Frayn reflects the risks and ambiguities of dramatising that lost moment by formally engaging with the very 'uncertainty principle' enshrined at the heart of quantum mechanics, and offers us two versions of that event, neither one presented as authoritatively 'true'. Equally, by stripping away all specifications of setting and showing the action as both a narrated event and something playing out before us, Frayn creates a haunting interplay between the form and content of the tale; this doubly layered narration, organised around motifs of arrival and departure and cunningly rhymed actions and gestures, seems to enable an event to play forward and backward at once. As Margrethe observes:

> ...I was there, and when I remember what it was like I'm there still, and I look around me and what I see isn't a story! It's confusion and rage and jealousy and tears and no one knowing what things mean or which way they're going to go.

So architectural form renders the elusiveness of memory visible in a manner far more striking than simple linguistic articulation.

The architect who designs a building that is complete in itself risks stifling the life and changes that human habitation will bring to their project; similarly, the impulse to play with form is a danger for a playwright. A play is a space to house a human story and must have give and, well, 'play' in it. To delight in form and plot to the exclusion of the unruliness of experience risks the lethal predictability of schematism – the characters subordinated to the elegance of the play's conceit. The best work of the playwright as architect is where there is a struggle between the elegance of the structure and the raw feeling of what it contains. *Copenhagen* risks that neatness, as does Ayckbourn's work; the patterns are sometimes all too clear, and predominate over the individual destinies being portrayed. But, just as some cultures build flaws into the body of their buildings, so the presence of Margrethe suggests the human cost of ideas, the idiosyncrasy of life beneath the architecture of great forms and concepts.

The Playwright as Poet

It might seem rash to conclude this discussion, and this book, with what could be seen as a tautology, the playwright as poet. After all, it was only in the Renaissance period that bald prose was first admitted onto the stage, and then largely as a means of indicating the lowly status of the character speaking it. But when considering the playwright as poet, poetry should not be seen as synonymous with verse. Poetry, in theatre as elsewhere, offers a more image-led logic than that which governs prose or everyday life. The playwright as poet is attentive to the power of words, of rhythm, and indeed fuses into a whole all the competencies outlined above and all the constituents of a play that have formed the subject of this book.

In some circles this is dangerous talk. For many, even to suggest that a play might be described in such a literary manner may put its real task in peril. Plays are about story, not poetry. Language is a means, not an end. For some the very adjective 'poetic' implies a lapse from the inherent virility of a play, its so-called muscularity. The poetic dramatist, like Narcissus, has fallen for their own voice, and the objective tasks of playwriting – architecture, sociology, journalism – have been problematically set aside.

Certainly, poets who turn to drama can make poor playwrights. It must be acknowledged that T.S. Eliot's plays, with the exception of *Murder in the Cathedral*, read better than they play, for all their hieratic power. Those now unstaged verse dramatists, the neo-Elizabethans who attempted to follow in his wake, from Christopher Fry to Ronald Duncan, became bywords for floridity.

I am suggesting a deeper notion of the poetic in playwriting, one that is linked to theatricality itself. To define it I want to end this account of plays with one of the greatest scenes in modern theatre, the penultimate scene of Brecht's *Mother Courage*. As noted previously, the play tracks its eponymous heroine's survival of the ravages of the most devastating war in German history before World War Two, a survival earned at the cost of the loss of her family. The last of her children to go is the mute Kattrin, who, in the scene 'The Stone Speaks', awakens the citizens of a sleeping town which is about to be invaded, by playing a drum on a rooftop to alert them to their imminent fate. The scene seems to be pushing us towards a sickeningly easy victory for the Ensign and soldiers, as they terrorise the peasants by threatening their cattle. The Peasant's Wife confirms this acquiescent fatalism as she abjures Kattrin to 'Pray, poor creature, pray! Nowt we can do to stop bloodshed' – and indeed sets out to pray herself whilst:

> Unobserved, KATTRIN *has slipped away to the cart and taken from it something she hides beneath her apron; then she climbs up the ladder to the stable roof.*

The poetry of the scene works in this sly juxtaposition – the prayer and the silent action thrillingly at odds with each other and pregnant with mystery.

I am not fluent enough in German to evaluate the power of this scene in its original language; but in fact, its language is strikingly functional. Most of the characters are nameless and new to the audience; the action takes its meaning from its contrast with the acerbic tenor of much of the rest of the play. The scene's quiet, devastating power comes from its concreteness, the fact that it stands almost in relief against the rest of the narrative. Here is an action that in itself can only end in futility; the fate of the peasants in the foreground is sealed, as is Kattrin's. But as she begins to drum, the scene acquires another poetic texture – the simple eloquence of non-verbal repetition lends the clumsy effort of the Ensign and the soldiers to silence her its own pathetic effect. As is so often the case with Brecht, the scene's full impact comes after it appears to have ended:

> THE ENSIGN. Set it up! Set it up! (*Calls up whilst the gun is being erected.*) For the very last time: stop drumming!
>
> KATTRIN, *in tears, drums as loud as she can.*
>
> Fire!
>
> *The* SOLDIERS *fire.* KATTRIN *is hit, gives a few more drumbeats and then slowly crumples.*
>
> That's the end of that.
>
> *But* KATTRIN's *last drumbeats are taken up by the town's cannon. In the distance can be heard the confused noise of tocsins and gunfire.*
>
> FIRST SOLDIER. She's made it.

Again, the detail here moves the scene beyond its function into something that has the resonance of great poetry: the Ensign taking care to offer Kattrin the chance to stop; the laboured efforts to assemble the gun; Kattrin's tears; her last enfeebled drumbeat standing in for her ebbing life; the suspension between the Ensign's ambivalent summation and the sound of a distant cannon, bells, shots – and then the brilliant tonal swerve of the First Soldier's unforced admiration for the woman he has killed.

The poet has one medium: language. The playwright has a battery of effects that can be articulated against each other: sound, silence, image, spatial level, character configuration, plotting. Thus the playwright as poet doesn't so much write actions as compose them, with the verbal complemented by the non-verbal, the implied space coexisting with the assembled bodies of the actors onstage. Brecht, of course, was a poet as well as a playwright; in this scene we see the two sensibilities triumphantly fused. Partially his poetic sense manifests itself in what we might call 'the feng shui' inherent in his scenic organisations – everything finds its most apposite and telling place, through the theatrical equivalent of Shelley's formulation of the art of poetry: 'the right words in the right order'. We see an event mapped out in offbeat sections across a split stage, with Kattrin above and the soldiers below – added to which is the offstage space of the sleeping town. All these forms of space interact in a way that is already akin to metaphor. Then we have the four forces of character in the scene: the passive farmers, the aggressive soldiers, the resistance of Kattrin, and the unseen population of the town (not to mention the absent mother herself). The scene's energy tugs between those four points of the compass to produce a moment of surpassing complexity, ushering in the poetic whilst not seeming to contrive it.

The poetic, then, is nothing other than the living aspect of the play itself; the realm in which the play escapes the will-power of the author and becomes more than it needs to be; the moment the play speaks to us unforgettably because, as in moments in life, it surprises us very deeply. Brecht, a notorious enemy of sentiment and a political cynic, a man who revelled in anti-heroism and who quoted with approval in *Galileo* the Chinese proverb 'Happy is the land without heroes', here gives us, in a play about survival, a scene of self-sacrificial heroism. The scene surely outstrips Brecht's apparent intentions and is full of the independent life evident in all great plays.

In this scene all the competencies of the playwright are demonstrated simultaneously: the playwright as sociologist draws on his past in rural Augsburg to capture the reticent manners of the farmers who sidestep conflict; the playwright as iconoclast constructs a scene that inverts the priorities of classical drama, granting all power to the non-speaking character, shifting attention at the climactic moment away from his protagonist, Mother Courage; the playwright as journalist shapes a searing image of resistance just as his nation succumbs to odious Fascism; the playwright as architect configures the scene to maximise its power in space and its emotional impact. But it is the fusion of all these competencies and knowledges that defines a playwright, yielding the poetic charge of a scene that remains in the memory long after it has played out and seems as vividly real as experiences in our own lives.

Coda

Hamlet lies dead on the stage, having pithily predicted that 'the rest is silence'. Fortinbras and the English Ambassadors come on to see the sprawled corpses of the Danish Court with only Horatio there to, as Hamlet puts it, 'report me and my cause aright'. The Ambassadors set the tone – they have turned up too late to announce the death of two minor characters, Rosencrantz and Guildenstern. One asks, bleakly, 'Where should we have our thanks?' Horatio deputises for the director, demanding that the dead be held up for view, 'high on a stage', and then wraps up the night with his account of what we have all apparently seen:

> So shall you hear
> Of carnal, bloody and unnatural acts,
> Of accidental judgements, casual slaughters,
> Of deaths put on by cunning and forc'd cause,
> And in this upshot, purposes mistook
> Fall'n on the inventors' heads...

Horatio's glib summary reveals why we need plays and what plays are. To reduce the rich, ambivalent events of the previous three hours to this paltry, moralised list; to draw general meanings from highly individualised actions; to hear no differentiation between Hamlet's acts and Claudius's, with all the dead muddled in the same bill of fare – this is almost as comically inept as something Polonius might have said. The action of *Hamlet*, like the action of any play that escapes from its author into independent life, defies a fifty-word précis.

Hamlet's account would have been quite different, as would Ophelia's, Laertes's, Gertrude's and so on – yet such is the exquisitely fashioned nature of the play that what transpires cannot be reduced to any one account, nor be described as any one thing. If there's any truth in Horatio's synopsis, it perhaps lies in the way it reflects on the writing of a play. 'Accidental judgements' is an oxymoron, but it might stand as an account of the way in which the playwright's decisions generate something that transcends conscious intent. '...purposes mistook / Fall'n on the inventors' heads' suggests, too negatively perhaps, how plays often exceed their makers' intentions – think of Ibsen stoutly demurring from the view that *A Doll's House* was a rallying call for the emancipation of women, or Brecht rewriting his plays to curb their emotional impact.

To conclude a book about playwriting by stating that the craft eludes definition, just as life itself defies summary, might seem perverse. But this discussion was always going to fall short of its subject matter, in the way that Horatio, who after all has been on the periphery of the story he describes, falls short. So for every observation about a particular play in this book, dozens of others lie in wait to contradict it; for every generalisation, a myriad of disobliging instances remain.

No one has ever got to the bottom of *Hamlet*. And because that is the case, the play and the character continue to live in their multifaceted, irregular, indefinable form. Likewise, having offered this account of the secret life of plays, for this writer at least, the mystery of playwriting has only deepened. Perhaps that mystery is the only thing that can finally be asserted with any confidence about how plays live.

Index

Titles of works are listed under author's name

THE SECRET LIFE OF PLAYS